Grace Is Not A Rocking Chair

Aaron Hopson

Copyright © 2005 Aaron Hopson
All rights reserved.

ISBN : 1-4196-1575-0

To order additional copies, please contact us.
BookSurge, LLC
www.booksurge.com
1-866-308-6235
orders@booksurge.com

Grace Is Not A Rocking Chair

Contents

1. Sound the Alarm — 1
2. The Power to be Kept — 9
3. The Salt of the Earth — 21
4. Battle Ready — 27
5. God's Plan of Salvation — 35
6. Forgiveness and Repentance — 49
7. Obedience is Essential — 77
8. Works Matter — 85
9. Choices and Accountability — 93
10. The Perils of Apostasy — 101
11. The Power Source — 121
12. The Importance of Tongues — 133
13. Breaking the Spirit of Lust — 141
14. Conclusion — 163
15. A Message to Christians — 169

To
God
Be
The
Glory

I dedicate this book to my Lord and Savior Jesus Christ, the only begotten Son of God. I thank you Lord Jesus for saving me from myself and granting me the privilege to proclaim your name, a mind to know and serve you and great expectation and hope as I await your glorious return.

Chapter One

Sound the Alarm

The purpose of this book is to sound the alarm for those that sleep and to exhort men to repentance and holiness. It is not an effort to push people out of the Kingdom of God, but rather a wake up call for the church to be true to the Word of God, and it's calling to be a holy nation, so that the world might see and follow its "light" and be saved.

As a church, we have become entertained by and accepting of sin, numb to guilt and conviction. We seek excuses and justifications for sin and are not being honest with God nor ourselves. Having adopted the standards of the world, we choose to sweep sin under the rug as opposed to attacking it and driving it out.

We sing and shout on Sunday morning and live comfortably in sin the moment we return home from service. In the confines of our homes, we enjoy the fruits of the world's lustful influences. We are proficient at wearing masks to hide the fact that we are no different than those in the world. At least the world knows who they are and don't profess to be righteous. We make Jesus look bad and crucify Him anew. It is time to turn back to God and come out from among them because God is not pleased. We are supposed to look and act like Him and not the world.

The Prophetic Dream

I found myself driving down the street with my wife and mother on a warm, breezy, sunny day. Everything appeared perfect including the beautiful blue, cloudless sky. The sun was so impressive that it seemed to fill the air with specks of light.

As I gazed upward, I saw a row of airplanes approaching looking like rubber pencils wobbling in the sky. As they got closer, they suddenly began falling with great speed. The pilots appeared to be making every attempt to pull up, but a powerful force seemed to be forcing them down. I was petrified as they began crashing to the ground one by one on the opposite side of the street. The force was such that they literally broke into a million pieces. There was smoke and fire everywhere as well as cars and buildings crushed by the planes.

One of the planes came so close that it clipped my truck and sent it tumbling over. Astonished that no one in the truck was hurt, we scrambled out and began running in fear along with hundreds of other people who had flooded the streets. There was utter confusion. Traffic had been brought to a halt as people abandoned their cars and ran for cover. Some were so stricken with fear that they dropped dead while others were crushed by falling debris. Dead bodies and body parts were stacked one on top of another and the streets were drenched with blood. The farther we ran the more the bodies littered the street.

Glancing again into the sky, I saw a dark red mist consume the sun and everything appeared to be covered by blood. I could hear people screaming in torment and pain. There was pink neon lightning that began streaking out of the sky followed by a loud cracking sound. We began to run again and I was suddenly engulfed by a bright white, blinding light. The light was so piercing that I lost track of everything else around me. I no longer saw my wife and mother who were running beside me. All I could do was look into the light and it was as if I was the only person in the world. I immediately knew to start praising the Lord. As I praised Him, I began to fade away and I understood that I was being raptured. Warmth encompassed me and totally consumed me.

I suddenly awoke out of my sleep and the Holy Spirit instructed me to start praying for my family, loved ones, and friends who had not given their lives to Jesus. I did as instructed and prayed that they would repent and surrender their lives to Him. He told me that His coming would be sudden and without notice, and those that had not surrendered their lives to Him would be lost.

Excerpt: "Why God Kept Saving Me"

The prophetic dream is a warning alerting us our Lord and Savior Jesus Christ will be returning soon and it is the calling of the church to prepare His way. It's not just a warning to those that are lost but also to those that claim to be found. The Lord is coming back for a church without spot or blemish. If His triumphant return was today what would He find? Has the way of the Lord been adequately prepared or have we, as a church, been lulled to sleep by a rocking chair mentality when it comes to God's grace? Are we, the bride of Christ, prepared for His coming, or are we simply a mirror image of the very world He came to deliver us out of?

We are living in the last days of the great story of God's love for man, and as it is written, we await the glorious return of our Lord and Savior Jesus Christ. As that day approaches, the Lord will continue to wake up His saints in order to prepare the way for His return. We must make the way of salvation known to the world. The gospel must be preached with purpose so all may have an opportunity to hear and receive the truth. It is not God's will that one man perish.

Be not deceived, the devil is also soliciting the minds of men, but with false doctrines that seduce and deceive God's people. He seeks to turn men away from God through disobedience and hardened hearts. Even in the church there are people that are being seduced into embracing disobedience, many times under the cover of grace. The end result is a heart that would rather enter through broad and wide gates into heaven, water down the word of God to accommodate disobedience, and embrace strange doctrines challenging the very foundations of Christianity. It's time to wake up and proclaim the truth for the day is at hand that all men will give an account of how they handled the grace of God.

Matthew 3:1-3

3:1 "In those days came John the Baptist, preaching in the wilderness of Judea,"

3:2 "And saying, Repent ye: for the kingdom of heaven is at hand."

3:3 "For this is he that was spoken of by the prophet Isaiah, saying, The voice of one crying in the wilderness, Prepare ye the way of the Lord, make His paths straight."

In order to prepare the way of the Lord, the body of Christ must rediscover the Word and will of God. It must accomplish its true purpose in the earth and be uncompromising in carrying out God's will.

It's Time to take heed to the Word of God

II Kings 22:8 "And Hilkiah the high priest said unto

Shaphan the scribe, I have found the book of the law in the house of the Lord. And Hilkiah gave the book to Shaphan, and he read it."

Once the word is discovered, we must be willing to seek the face of the Lord, repent, and turn from our wicked ways. The church as a whole must repent of its shortcomings, complacency, and idleness. We must stop attempting to bring the word down to us and have the humility to change our behavior and attitudes to line up with it.

<u>II Kings 22:10-13</u>
22:10 "And Shaphan the scribe shewed the king saying, Hilkiah the priest hath delivered me a book. And Shaphan read it before the king."
22:11 "And it came to pass, when the king had heard the words of the book of the law, that he rent his clothes."
22:12 " And the king commanded Hilkiah the priest, and Ahikam the son of Shaphan, and Achbor the son of Michaiah, and Shaphan the scribe, and Asahiah a servant of the king's saying,"
22:13 "Go ye, enquire of the Lord for me, and for all the people, and for all Judah, concerning the words of this book that is found: for great is the wrath of the Lord that is kindled against us, because our fathers have not hearkened unto the words of this book, to do according unto all that which is written concerning us."

The Lord is faithful to those that call out on His name from a pure heart. A heart of repentance brings about a good conscience towards God and boldness in the faith. When we justify our sins, we alienate God by reasoning away His commandments. We numb our hearts to conviction by explaining away our conscience and rationalizing our sin.

II Kings 22:18-20

22:18 "But to the king of Judah which sent you to enquire of the Lord, thus shall ye say to him, Thus saith the Lord God of Israel, As touching the words which thou hast heard."

22:19 "Because thine heart was tender, and thou hast humbled thyself before the Lord, when thou heardest what I spake against this place, and against the inhabitants thereof, that they should become a desolation and a curse, and hast rent thy clothes, and wept before me; I also have heard thee, saith the Lord."

22:20 "Behold therefore, I will gather thee unto thy fathers, and thou shalt be gathered into thy grave in peace; and thine eyes shall not see all the evil which I will bring upon this place. And they brought the king word again."

You must have a made up mind and make a firm decision to live by the Word of God. This requires a commitment to be uncompromising, non-complacent, and steadfast when it comes to the things of God.

Obey God's Commandments Rather Than Men

The Bible is not a book of suggestions. Rather it is a mandate for having a relationship with God through our Lord and Savior Jesus Christ and living a victorious life. It's also an invitation to mercy and grace to those that seek it, lessons to model our lives after, and warnings to those that oppose God's instruction. The Bible is a complete document that is either 100% right or 100% wrong. You either believe that it is divinely inspired by God or merely written by men. It is a road map to salvation, or simply a book of poems, fables, and opinions.

II Timothy 3:16-17

3:16 "All scripture is given by inspiration of God, and

is profitable for doctrine, for reproof, for correction, for instruction in righteousness:"

3:17 "That the man of God may be perfect, thoroughly furnished unto all good works."

God's standard is very different from our standard and He is not moved by compromise and negotiation. The Bible states in Proverbs 14:12 "There is a way which seemeth right unto a man, but the end thereof are the ways of death." The true test of loving the Lord is not measured by attending church service, telling others you love the Lord, or wearing a "what would Jesus do" wristband. The true test of love, as defined by our Lord and Savior Jesus Christ, is to keep His commandments.

The Bible says a relationship with Jesus is defined by a person's lifestyle and not his rhetoric. Only in the world does talking a good game count for something. In the body of Christ, your actions give meaning to the true intent, motive, and sincerity of your words. The devil infiltrates the church and can even quote scriptures, but the one thing he can't do is obey the commandments of God and follow the lifestyle of Jesus Christ. If Jesus is truly on the inside, then you have been empowered to live the life that He led.

Covenant relationship:
II Kings 23:3 "And the king stood by a pillar, and made a covenant before the Lord, to walk after the Lord, and to keep His commandments and His testimonies and His statutes with all their heart and all their soul, to perform the words of this covenant that were written in this book. And all the people stood to the covenant."

A covenant relationship with God is a firm decision

to choose the things of God over the things in the world. You are committed to following God's way as opposed to the worlds. You commit your heart, soul, mind, body, and Spirit to God by making a choice to serve Him and obey His statutes and commandments. You are willing to line your life up with His Word and live a life that is pleasing in His sight. You put nothing before Him whether it is people, circumstances, or material things.

This does not mean you are going to be perfect, or there will be no battles to fight. There will even be times you miss the mark, but a covenanted person is honest with himself and with God. You have undertaken a journey to discover the things of God, learn how to trust Him, and live by His Word to the best of your ability. You have a heart to make your wrongs right and take the necessary steps to avoid repeating the wrong. You put yourself in position to be used by God, share His goodness with others and restore godliness in this world.

Chapter Two

The Power to be Kept

There are those that have the mistaken notion that "once saved, always saved." In other words, their salvation is sealed once they give their lives to Jesus Christ. All they have to do is sit back and wait on Jesus to burst through the clouds or simply die first. This is a nice thought but without surrendering your life to God, it is nothing more than a catch phrase. It does not take into account that we can allow our minds to become reprobate by choosing to chase after the things of this world and refusing to live by God's word. A better notion would be "once saved, you can be kept."

<u>Revelation 21:6-8</u>
21:6 "And He said unto me, It is done. I am Alpha and Omega, the beginning and the end. I will give unto him that is athirst of the fountain of the water of life freely."

21:7 "He that overcometh shall inherit all things; and I will be his God, and he shall be my son."

21:8 "But the fearful, and unbelieving, and whoremongers, and sorcerers, and idolaters, and all liars, shall have their part in the lake which burneth with fire and brimstone: which is the second death."

The Lord will, in fact, return and the choice is yours whether or not you will be ready when He comes. Throughout this book, scriptures will support the fact God can save you and keep you once you're saved, but it is an individual choice to be kept. The way of the Lord must be prepared so all men have an opportunity to make that choice and be ready for His return.

Since the fall of man, God had spoken a plan of salvation for every man, woman, and child to be redeemed back to Him. This plan incorporated a means by which each of us could achieve this end. Within this plan the road to Heaven had already been paved, our Savior had already been prepared, our mansions in Heaven had already been built, our callings and purposes had been predetermined, the rapture date set, and preparations were finalized for the marriage supper of the Lamb. A chair was placed at the table of the feast for every man, woman, and child, but it was conditioned upon choice and free will.

The key here can be summed up in one word "choice." Choice adds meaning to the human experience, and is the one thing distinguishing man from the rest of God's creatures. God entrusted man with the awesome responsibility to choose his own fate.

God spoke His perfect will into the earth including what He purposed to accomplish, and what would come to pass, but God's perfect will has always been conditioned upon man's right to choose. This is the "free moral agent clause" written into every promise. This clause states that we never lose the right to choose whether or not to come into agreement with God's will.

Do you think it was the will of God for Adam to disobey Him in the garden or for Moses to strike the rock instead of speaking to it in the wilderness? Do you think it was the will of God for King David to sleep with Bathsheba and conspire to have her husband killed? Of course not, but man's dominion in the earth includes his sovereign right to choose. His right to choose superseded the perfect will of God because he was afforded this right.

Because all men are born in sin, there is a predisposition to make the wrong choices in our lives, but God, through Jesus Christ, granted us power to choose right by making supernatural love available. Every person has access to this supernatural love. This love is not the result of coercion, bribery, or domination, but rather choice and free will. God wanted a family that would choose to love Him as opposed to robots that simply carry out programmed instructions.

By choosing Jesus Christ as our Lord and Savior, we have made a choice to dwell in His love. It is His love that draws our obedience, drives us to repentance, and keeps us faithfully striving in the word and prayer. As long as we choose to dwell in love, we can be kept because this love causes us to seek His will as opposed to our own. Despite the pleasures and allurements of sin, our attitude must be *I still choose you Lord because I love you. Even if it means I have to give up certain things, change my lifestyle, or make sacrifices, I am willing and obedient Lord because none of these things can compare to the love I have for you!*

A. **To be kept you must live by the word of God.** Jesus Christ is the word made flesh and it produces life, victory, joy and power to name a few of its attributes. His word is our blueprint to Heaven and to live contrary to God's blueprint results in devastation, loss, and ultimately destruction. You cannot separate God from His word. Throughout the Bible God warns us and rewards us. If you are going to be kept, the Word of God is essential in your life.

Psalm 19:7-8
19:7 "The law of the Lord is perfect, converting the soul: the testimony of the Lord is sure, making the wise simple."
19:8 "The statutes of the Lord are right, rejoicing the heart: the commandment of the Lord is pure, enlightening the eyes."

B. You can be kept by the Holy Ghost.
John 14:26 "But the Comforter, which is the Holy Ghost, whom the Father will send in my name, He shall teach you all things, and bring all things to your remembrance, whatsoever I have said unto you."

John 16:13 "Howbeit when He, the Spirit of Truth, is come, He will guide you into all truth: for He shall not speak of Himself; but whatsoever He shall hear, that shall He speak: and He will show you things to come."

Ephesians 1:13
1:13 "In whom ye also trusted, after that ye heard the word of truth, the gospel of your salvation in whom ye also, after that ye believed, ye were sealed with that Holy Spirit of promise."

II Corinthians 1:21-22
1:21 "Now He which stablisheth us with you in Christ, and hath anointed us, is God."
1: 22 "Who hath also sealed us, and given the earnest of the Spirit in our hearts."

C. You can be kept through confidence and faith in God.

Philippians 1:6 "Being confident of this very thing, that he which hath begun a good work in you will perform it until the day of Jesus Christ"

Philippians 2:13 "For it is God which worketh in you both to will and to do His good pleasure."

I Thessalonians 5:24 "Faithful is he that calleth you, who also will do it."

II Thessalonians 2:16-17
2:16 "Now our Lord Jesus Christ Himself, and God, even our Father, which hath loved us, and hath given us everlasting consolation and good hope through grace,"
2:17 "Comfort your hearts, and stablish you in every good word and work."

II Thessalonians 3:3
3:3 "But the Lord is faithful, who shall stablish you, and keep you from evil."

I Peter 1:3-5
1:3 "Blessed be the God and Father of our Lord Jesus Christ, which according to His abundant mercy hath begotten us again unto a lively hope by the resurrection of Jesus Christ from the dead. "
1:4 "To an inheritance incorruptible, and undefiled, and that fadeth not away, reserved in Heaven for you."
1: 5 "Who are kept by the power of God through faith unto salvation ready to be revealed in the last time."

I Peter 4:19 "Wherefore let them that suffer according to the will of God commit the keeping of their souls to Him in well doing, as unto a faithful Creator."

D. You can be kept through separation from the world system:

Mark 10:29-30

10:29 "And Jesus answered and said, Verily I say unto you, There is no man that hath left house, or brethren, or sisters, or father, or mother, or wife, or children, or lands, for my sake, and the gospel's,

10: 30 "But he shall receive an hundredfold now in this time, houses, and brethren, and sisters, and mothers, and children, and lands, with persecutions, and in the world to come eternal life."

John 17:14-16

17:14 "I have given them thy word; and the world hath hated them, because they are not of the world, even as I am not of the world."

17: 15 "I pray not that thou shouldest take them out of the world, but that thou shouldest keep them from the evil."

17:1 16 "They are not of the world, even as I am not of the world."

The Bible warns us to be separate from the world's way of doing things. We must be willing to die to the old man, or the old characteristics and ways of thinking, and make a firm decision not to partake in those activities that are ungodly or can lead to ungodliness. You can not act like the world, think like the world, or party with the world and stay in fellowship with God.

Living for Christ is a decision to align yourself with

the things of God and no longer participate in behaviors that oppose, contradict, diminish, and discredit God's Word. It is a choice not to compromise the things of God regardless of the tough decisions that have to be made, people you may disappoint, or events that you may miss.

The more you grow in Christ and learn about His nature, the more selective you are about where you go, what you listen to, and who you hang around. That is why it is every Christian's responsibility to learn more about God, spend time with Him in the Word and prayer, and develop a personal relationship with Him.

<u>I John 2:15-17</u>
2:15 "Love not the world, neither the things that are in the world. If any man love the world, the love of the Father is not in him"

2: 16 "For all that is in the world, the lust of the flesh, and the lust of the eyes, and the pride of life, is not of the Father, but is of the world"

2: 17 "And the world passeth away, and the lust thereof: but he that doeth the will of God abideth forever"

<u>II Corinthians 6 14-18</u>
6:14 "Be ye not unequally yoked together with unbelievers: for what fellowship hath righteousness with unrighteousness? and what communion hath light with darkness?"

6: 15 "And what concord hath Christ with Belial? or what part hath he that believeth with an infidel?"

6: 16 "And what agreement hath the temple of God with idols? For ye are the temple of the living God; as God hath said, I will dwell in them, and I will be their God, and they shall be my people"

6: 17 "Wherefore come out from among them, and be ye separate, saith the Lord, and touch not the unclean thing; and I will receive you."

6: 18 "And will be a Father unto you, and ye shall be my sons and daughters, saith the Lord Almighty"

Ephesians 5:11 "And have no fellowship with the unfruitful works of darkness, but rather reprove them"

There is no peace in the world for a child of God because the spirit of the world recognizes who you are, and knows you don't belong. The Spirit within you is in direct opposition with the spirit that is in the world. When Jesus came across people possessed by the devil, the demonic spirits in them already knew who He was. In other words, worldly spirits will increasingly despise you because of the Christ in you. Demons recognize the Spirit of Christ and will work even harder to rob you of your peace and ultimately your soul. Have you ever wondered why it seems like people in the world boldly do ungodly things and have the times of their lives, but the moment you try, it results in disastrous consequences? A child of God only has the illusion of fitting in the world.

Mark 1:23-24
1:23 "And there was in the synagogue a man with an unclean spirit; and he cried out,"

1:24 "Saying, Let us alone; what have we to do with thee, thou Jesus of Nazareth? Art thou come to destroy us? I know thee who thou art, the Holy one of God."

Mark 3:11 "And unclean spirits, when they saw Him,

fell down before Him, and cried, saying, Thou art the Son of God."

E. **You can be kept by renewing your mind:**
Romans 12:2 "And be not conformed to this world: but be ye transformed by the renewing of your mind, that ye may prove what is good, and acceptable, and perfect, will of God."

Renewing the mind involves surrendering our thoughts, beliefs, and ideas to God. Each born again Christian is given the opportunity to embrace and nurture the character of Christ. The more we pray, take in the Word of God, and surround ourselves with Godly influences, the more we take on His character.

Mind renewal is a process in truth that allows us to shed the lies, deception, and ungodly influences that we embraced before surrendering our lives to Christ. Failure to renew the mind ultimately results in back sliding, or reverting back to old ways. The more we die to the things of the world, the more alive we become in the things of God. God's way and the world's way are in direct opposition, which makes it impossible to be neutral or straddle the fence. The more you engage in worldly activity the more you confuse, frustrate, and fail to retain the things of God. Mind renewal is the end result of separation from the world.

Ephesians 2:2 "Wherein in time past ye walked according to the course of this world, according to the prince of the power of the air, the spirit that now worketh in the children of disobedience"

II Corinthians 5:17 "Therefore if any man be in Christ, he is a new creature: old things are passed away; behold, all things are become new."

Ephesians 4:24 "And that ye put on the new man, which after God is created in righteousness and true holiness."

Colossians 3:10 "And have put on the new man, which is renewed in knowledge after the image of Him that created him."

Ephesians 4:17-18
4:17 "This I say therefore, and testify in the Lord, that ye henceforth walk not as other Gentiles walk, in the vanity of their mind."
18 "Having the understanding darkened, being alienated from the life of God through the ignorance that is in them, because of the blindness of their heart."

Ephesians 4:22-24
4:22 "That ye put off concerning the former conversation the old man, which is corrupt according to the deceitful lusts."
4:23 "And be renewed in the spirit of your mind."
4:24 "And that ye put on the new man, which after God is created in righteousness and true holiness."

The good news is that if you are willing to do your part your salvation can be assured. You can know that you know that you know that you are saved and can live a life free from condemnation and guilt. You can look forward to heaven and have no doubt about your being there. You can have liberty and peace in knowing that you are one of

His special ambassadors in whom He is well pleased. You won't have to question your salvation every time you mess up because you will have confidence in the fact you are in a covenant relationship with God who is faithful and totally in control.

Chapter Three

The Salt of the Earth

The Lord will undeniably return and the choice is yours whether or not you will be ready when He comes. In fact, God made a way for every man, woman, and child to be ready for His return. He put everything in place including His word, a 24 hour prayer line, the Holy Ghost, and fire insurance (the opportunity to repent). He even prepared churches, preachers, evangelists, prophets, apostles, missionaries, and other willing workers to prepare the way for His return. It is the very nature of God to call those things that be not as though they were, and salvation is no exception.

The church's responsibility is to lead the way through God's Word and its examples. The unadulterated Word of God must be preached just as hard to those professing to be Christian as to the lost. The church cannot assume it is fulfilling the mandate of God simply because people claim to be Christians, especially when their lifestyles are oftentimes saying something else.

Ezekiel 33:31-32
33:31 "And they come unto thee as the people cometh, and they sit before thee as my people, and they hear thy words, but will not do them: for with their mouth

they shew much love, but their heart goeth after their covetousness."

33: 32 " And, lo, thou art unto them as a very lovely song of one that hath a pleasant voice, and can play well on an instrument: for they hear thy words, but they do them not."

The church must be uncompromising in its stance against sin, clear concerning the judgment of God, and focused on discipleship and obedience to God's Word. If we fail to do so, there will be a significant number of professing Christians who are going to receive the shock of their lives when they stand before God. God is not pleased with disobedience and worldliness, and as believers, we are responsible to teach and live our lives in such a way that all men will know the truth.

The Bible warns us that the day would come that men would no longer adhere to sound doctrine choosing rather to hear only those things that satisfied their flesh. We are in that day and more and more professing Christians are mistakenly abandoning the Word of God and traveling down roads of deviation.

There used to be a time when a Christian was just that- a Christian. People generally knew where you stood because the Bible was seen as cut and dry. They expected you to live, act, and treat others a certain way. It was easy to identify hypocrisy because people relied on the yea and nay of the word. Today some Christians don't even know what the title Christian truly means because the devil has been very effective at destroying their identity and promoting a rocking chair mentality when it comes to the grace of God. What does it mean when you say that you're a Christian but your lifestyle is identical to someone that is not? What does it mean to say that you're a Christian but you don't believe in the Bible? Is being a Christian simply a title or declaration, or does it signify a relationship with responsibility?

We find doctrines that change depending on which building you walk in. In one building you may find amazing grace and in another you may find a service that reminds you of a talent show. We have danced and sang for the world, embraced their culture, and even embraced wordily icons all in the name of trying to entertain souls to Christ. The result is a divided church with countless interpretations of the same sentence. It's time for us to ask the question. **Did Jesus become like the world to win the world or did Jesus preach and demonstrate change in a dying world?**

The Bible instructs us to come out of the world because God knew all to well the effect the world would have on the heart. When Christians play on both sides of the fence, take the grace of God for granted, practice sin, and fail to spend time with God in the word and prayer, they are in danger of losing the supernatural love that seals their relationship with Him.

The root of all hypocrisy is the attitude that one can willfully engage in the pleasures of sin while claiming to be a Christian. I use the term willfully to distinguish those that are babies in Christ from those that know to do right but still choose to do wrong. Some people sin because they are weak and others because they want too. A weak Christian makes every attempt to turn away from sin but simply falls short, whereas a disobedient person sins because he has made a decision to enjoy the pleasures of sin. Too many Christians are hiding in the land of willingly ignorant where we have revelation, but simply refuse to give up the inappropriate behavior or accept what the word says on the issue. When you have a genuine love for God, and a surrendered heart you choose Him above everything else.

Jeremiah 7:8-10

7:8 "Behold, ye trust in lying words, that cannot profit."

7:9 "Will ye steal, murder, and commit adultery, and swear falsely, and burn incense unto Baal, and walk after other gods whom ye know not."

7:10 "And come and stand before me in this house, which is called by my name, and say, We are delivered to do all these abominations?"

We must get back to operating by the word of God, and Christians must once again follow only the examples of Christ. Christ must be the beginning and the end for everyone that professes He is their savior. You are not a Christian because you profess Christ, but because you follow Christ. The Bible is the final word for Christians and those that denounce the Bible are not Christians.

The biggest threat to Christianity is allowing the world to define for us what Christianity means. Since when did Christians not live according to the Bible? Now we see people who are quick to challenge the Bible, rewrite the Bible, and question its validity, rather than simply obey it. We see others that take the position that God's love supersedes His commandments as opposed to accepting that God's love is His commandment. God's love is inviting not accommodating. You either accept it under the condition it is offered or you reject it.

One of the methods Satan uses to discredit Christianity is attacking and distorting the image of God's love in order to hinder the body of Christ. The closer we get to the Lord's return, the harder he works to destroy, discredit, and undermine the very foundations of Christianity. He wages around the clock warfare to separate us from God's word, strip Biblical principals away from our institutions, portray

Christians as insensitive hate mongers, and changing the very identity of what it means to be a Christian. We must not allow Satan or society define for us what being a Christian means. Daily he is busy drawing people away from the true love of God and seducing them into sin and ungodliness.

Christians can no longer allow the world to distort God's Word and change His standards to accommodate their choices. The Word must be preached as an invitation out of sin and not compromised in order to be politically correct or inclusive. The Bible is not an inclusive book. You are either following God's instruction or you're not.

Premeditating sin and being willfully ignorant to God's instruction must stop. You must be open to chastisement and correction even when it requires you to change something about yourself. You will make fewer mistakes and daily grow stronger and stronger in the revelation of God. This produces humility as opposed to being quick fused, impatient, and defensive. You will become a living billboard others can see that is not clouded by contradiction and hypocrisy. Your actions will be consistent with your words because of the goodness in your heart, but most of all you will be able to say you're a Christian, and others will know exactly what that means.

<u>Matthew 5:13-16</u>
5:13 "Ye are the salt of the earth: but if the salt have lost his savor? Wherewith shall it be salted? It is thenceforth good for nothing, but to be cast out, and to be trodden under foot of men."

5:14 "Ye are the light of the world. A city that is set on an hill cannot be hid."

5:15 "Neither do men light a candle, and put it under

a bushel, but on a candlestick; and it giveth light unto all that are in the house."

5:16 "Let your light so shine before men, that they may see your good works, and glorify your Father which is in heaven."

Chapter Four

Battle Ready

I John 4:16-17
4:16 "And we have known and believed the love that God hath to us. God is love; and he that dwelleth in love dwelleth in God, and God in him."

4:17 "Herein is our love made perfect, that we may have boldness in the Day of Judgment: because as He is, so are we in this world."

The essence of everything we do as Christians is driven by the love of God which is available to all men regardless of color, gender, sexual orientation, lifestyle, or ethnic background. Through this love, we dwell in the presence of the Lord and manifest His will in the earth. The assignment of every Christian is to share God's love with others and publish the good news of the gospel. The Bible does not instruct us to use hate, condemnation, and intimidation simply because others don't agree; rather it is an invitation that can be accepted or rejected. If people choose not to believe, we must continue to show them love while standing firm in our convictions, and never compromising the Word of God to accommodate their beliefs. As Christians, the word of God, the Bible, is the standard by which we live. Jesus did not use His power to destroy His enemies; He used His compassion to save them and His love to forgive them. Those that use hate to battle against sin are not operating in God's love.

Luke 9:54-56
9:54 "And when His disciples James and John saw this, they said, Lord, wilt thou that we command fire to come down from Heaven, and consume them, even as Elias did?
9:55 "But He turned, and rebuke them, and said, Ye know not what manner of Spirit ye are of."
9:56 "For the Son of Man is not come to destroy men's lives, but to save them. And they went to another village."

The love of God is not an excuse to live outside of His will, or a cloak for our unwillingness to let go of those things we cling so tightly to in the world. The more God's Word is diminished, the more we embrace a standard for love which is inclusive of man's desire as opposed to God's will.

God's love draws us to repentance and closer to Him not further into the world and sin. More and more people are distorting the meaning of His love to justify living outside of His will. They use phrases such as "God loves me the way I am", or "God loves me too much to send me to hell," as an excuse to remain in sin. Biblical love is not defined this way. The Bible says God hates sin and through His love He made a way out of sin whose end result is death and eternal separation from God. If a person refuses to exercise his right to escape sin, then it is not the love of God that brings about eternal separation. It is the individual that has chosen the consequences of hell over the invitation to life.

There is no greater love than the sacrifice of God in giving His only begotten son, Jesus Christ, to die on the cross for our sins. He did not die so that we could continue being a part of the world system and live outside of His will. He died so men could escape the curse of sin which results in death, poverty, sickness, and eternal separation from God. The Lord came as a sword to divide those that accept Him from those that choose to remain in the world. He came to deliver His brethren out of the world, not leave them in.

Ephesians 4:17-19
4:17 "This I say therefore, and testify in the Lord, that ye henceforth walk not as other Gentiles walk, in the vanity of their mind."

4:18 "Having the understanding darkened, being alienated from the life of God through the ignorance that is in them, because of the blindness of their heart."

4:19 "Who being past feeling have given themselves over unto lasciviousness, to work all uncleanness with greediness"

God is not the one that alienates us. We alienate ourselves from the things of God by making a decision to remain in darkness as opposed to the light and revelation of the Word of God.

Matthew 10:38 "And he that taketh not his cross, and followeth after me, is not worthy of me."

It is not God's will anyone perish, but that all would come to repentance. The Bible says in John 8:32 "And ye shall know the truth and the truth shall make you free." The unadulterated word of God must be preached even if it means smaller congregations and greater persecution from the world around us. Even if the congregation is smaller, the manifestation of God's power will be bigger.

The issue is not so much the message being preached on Sunday mornings, but rather the message being seen Monday thru Saturday. The Bible says in II Corinthians 3:2 "we are living epistles known and read of all men." God's plan was that the world would be won and convicted through the light of His people. We are supposed to be ministering each and everyday the words of God through our actions, conversation, and lifestyles. The world is not only supposed to see how blessed we are, but how holy we are as well. We are quick to proclaim the scriptures that designate us as prosperous above all people, but are increasingly ignoring the call to be a holy nation zealous of good works. When we live like grace is a license to sin, that is the message we proclaim to the world, and more and more people are becoming progressively turned off by this blatant hypocrisy. We are giving Satan significantly more territory than he is taking by advertising junk and justifying garbage.

We must stop looking for loopholes and technicalities to enter into heaven. It's time to be about our Father's business and quit hiding behind titles, catch phrases, and religion. The word of God must again be the standard that unites us in the faith making us consistent in the voice we present to the world. Our leaders must lead by example, practice what they preach, and speak with less opinion and more scripture. Members must develop a personal relationship with God through the word and prayer and stop waiting for someone to spoon-feed it to them. We must all be mindful to win souls, and allow our lights to shine brightly in the world.

John 15:18-19

15:18 "If the world hate you, ye know that it hated me before it hated you."

15:19 "If ye were of the world, the world would love his own: but because ye are not of the world, but I have chosen you out of the world, therefore the world hateth you."

Professing Christians must stop hiding behind the phrase "only God can judge me," in order to avoid being held accountable for their actions and having the answer of a good conscience. The Bible instructs us to know a man by his fruits, or actions, which is the positive side to judgment, as opposed to criticism, and condemnation, which is the negative side. God has even made the gift of discerning spirits available in order to help us judge what manner of spirit we are dealing with. The key to judging is to judge according to what the word says and not based on our opinion and perceptions.

The devil wants nothing more than for Christians to stop discerning the fruits of an individual so he can have free course to deceive, infiltrate, manipulate, confuse, frustrate, divide, and ultimately conquer the body of Christ. This is why God wants us to know one another so we can pray for those that are lost. We are to pray first and then be led by the Holy Spirit in order to love that individual back to Christ.

The Bible also warns us to be aware of wolves in sheep's clothing. If you act like a wolf, then you are a wolf. Pray the wolf out of the individual first and then receive him as a "sheep." A wolf should not be the pastor of the church, the choir director, youth director, a deacon, or hold other important offices others look to for an example. I'm not saying a person cannot repent and be restored. I am merely stating that wisdom should be used and a person given time to demonstrate through his actions that he is restored. Allow others to see the new fruit as opposed to giving the impression that sin is simply swept under the rug. Exceptions should not be made for those that continue to practice sin.

We must stop allowing our children to be influenced by worldly people seeking to devour their minds simply because they get up and say "I would like to thank my Lord and Savior Jesus Christ" while receiving their worldly awards. We must be discernable of those individuals our kids look to as role models. If you allow your children to be bombarded with sexual images and rebellious overtones, then quit acting surprised when you find out they're having sex, or have no respect for, or interest in the things of God.

Matthew 7:15-20

7:15 "Beware of false prophets, which come to you in sheep's clothing, but inwardly they are ravening wolves."

7:16 "Ye shall know them by their fruits. Do men gather grapes of thorns, or figs of thistles?"

7:17 "Even so every good tree bringeth forth good fruit; but a corrupt tree bringeth forth evil fruit."

7:18 "A good tree cannot bring forth evil fruit, neither can a corrupt tree bring forth good fruit."

7:19 "Every tree that bringeth not forth good fruit is hewn down and cast into the fire."

7:20 "Wherefore by their fruits ye shall know them."

The time is now to live according to God's Word. Our commission is to prepare the way of the Lord by demonstrating God's Word and instructing people in righteousness, in order that they might be ready to stand before God. The Lord is coming back for His bride soon, and as that day approaches the Word of God must be preached in the earth with deliberate intent. We must alert people that although uttering a few words at the alter is a good first step, the decisions that are made after they confess Christ are equally important. We cannot water down the word to avoid offending people or condone living on both sides of the fence. The day is at hand that the body of Christ will not be defined by titles, church affiliation, outward success, status, or any other standards of men. Those that love the Lord and keep His commandments will define the body of Christ and they shall be comprised of many different walks of life.

The Bible says in Matthew 19:30 "But many that are first shall be last; and the last shall be first." The measure of our work is not in big buildings, material success, and the admiration of men because the day comes when all those things shall be destroyed. It's not about the outward show; it is about the inward condition. We are in a time of war and we must do everything we can to ensure each man, woman, and child is ready to stand before the Lord.

A man once told me "If you are going to be holy, then be holy, otherwise shut up and drink your beer because even the world hates a hypocrite." We, as Christians, need to either live the life that Christ led, or quit trying to teach others about Christ. People do not hear what you say as much as they watch what you do. There is so much hypocrisy in the world today that to simply say you're Christian means very little to people. Too many people use the word Christian as an excuse for sin and a justification for Heaven. The world has numerous examples of people that use the title whose lifestyle is virtually identical to theirs.

The body of Christ can no longer afford to engage in

shadow boxing when it comes to dealing with the enemy, meaning we are on fire for God as long as a real opponent isn't standing in front of us. On Sunday mornings, we stomp on the devil's head and declare he is under our feet, but Monday thru Saturday we are powerless to effect any real change in our communities, our homes, or the lives of others. We can't even battle a cigarette or a beer bottle on Friday. We tell the Lord we are faithful to death, but continue to engage in fornication. We are quick to confess our love for Christ, but refuse to love one another.

We sing the song "We are soldiers in the army of the Lord," but spend the bulk of our time enjoying carnal pleasure behind enemy lines. We are not prepared to battle sin, endure hardship, or handle setbacks. The reality is that in any battle there will be casualties, plans that go wrong, moments you are outsmarted by your enemy, times you must tend to your wounds, intense gun fights, and outcomes which are unexpected. A Christian soldier puts on the whole armor of God and is prepared through the word and prayer for bullet wounds, fatigue, tough fights, and other traits that are associated with battle.

It's time for the body of Christ to count up the cost and become the army God called us to be. He will accept whoever comes and there will be those that are exalted in the eyes of men that shall be abased by God, and those that are rejected in the eyes of men that the Lord will exalt. It's time to be Battle Ready and make His paths straight!

I Peter 2:9 "But ye are a chosen generation, a royal priesthood, an holy nation, peculiar people; that ye should shew forth the praises of Him who hath called you out of darkness into His marvelous light:"

Chapter Five

God's Plan of Salvation

Romans 10:9-10
10:9 "That if thou shalt confess with thy mouth the Lord Jesus, and shalt believe in thine heart that God hath raised him from the dead, thou shalt be saved."
10:10 "For with the heart man believeth unto righteousness; and with the mouth confession is made unto salvation"

There is absolutely nothing you must do to receive salvation other than exercising (1)your faith to believe on the work of the cross, (Jesus Christ, the Son of God, died on the cross for our sins, arose from the dead, and is now seated on the throne of God), (2) your mouth to make your confession of belief (confessing that Jesus Christ, the Son of God, died for your sins and your belief in Him as your Lord and savior), (3) and your heart to receive Jesus Christ as your personal Lord and savior.

John 6:37 "All that the Father giveth me shall come to me; and him that cometh to me I will in no wise cast out."

The Bible tells us you can come to Jesus as you are and He will in no wise cast you out. The way to God has been paved by His plan of salvation which is a free gift made possible through faith in Jesus Christ. It has nothing to do with the character or condition of the individual asking for it; rather it is a condition of the heart mixed with an expression of faith. It is God's will that men be saved and the whole purpose of ministry is to win souls to Jesus.

Ephesians 2:8 "For by grace are ye saved through faith; and that not of yourselves: it is the gift of God."

Salvation has been offered to all through God's grace and mercy.

Romans 6:23 "For the wages of sin is death; but the gift of God is eternal life through Jesus Christ our Lord"

II Corinthians 9:15 "Thanks be unto God for His unspeakable gift."

Because salvation has been made available to all men, it is a universal call uniting and restoring us back to our inheritance. He has offered us a way of escape and provided a plan of restoration when we fall.

Luke 3:6 "And all flesh shall see the salvation of God"

Acts 2:21 "And it shall come to pass that whosoever shall call on the name of the Lord shall be saved."

Romans 10:13 "For whosoever shall call upon the name of the Lord shall be saved."

The Bible is very clear on this. Anyone can be saved. Yet, the question still remains—what happens after you have received salvation? Some argue that the one time expression of faith and belief in the Lord as savior covers them to eternity, regardless of the condition of the individual's heart from that point on. The only problem with that assertion is that the scriptures clearly indicate there is more involved once salvation is received.

The Bible is our blueprint to Heaven after we receive Jesus Christ as our Lord and Savior. He is the word made flesh and when we make a decision to accept Him we are making a decision to adhere to His Word. We cannot separate the decision to accept Jesus from the responsibility to adhere to His Word. Jesus is the living Word and it is the Word that sustains us once we are saved.

John 1:1-2, 14
1:1 "In the beginning was the Word, and the Word was with God, and the Word was God."
1:2 "The same was in the beginning with God."
1:14 "And the Word was made flesh, and dwelt among us, (and we beheld His glory, the glory as of the only begotten of the Father,) full of grace and truth."

The following are some components of salvation, and each will be examined in more detail in later chapters:

1. Confession: You must continue to confess Jesus Christ as your Lord and Savior.

Luke 12:8-9
12:8 "Also I say unto you, Whosoever shall confess me before men, him shall the Son of Man also confess before the angels of God."

12:9 "But he that denieth me before men shall be denied before the angels of God."

2. Belief:

Acts 10:43 "To Him give all the prophets witness, that through His name whosoever believeth in Him shall receive remission of sins."

3. Faith: You must continue to have faith in God and since faith and the word are connected, you must continue to have a relationship with the word of God.

Hebrews 11:6 "But without faith it is impossible to please Him: for he that cometh to God must believe that He is, and that He is a rewarder of them that diligently seek Him."

Romans 10:17 "So then faith cometh by hearing, and hearing by the word of God."

4. Endurance: You must make a decision to endure until the end.

Matthew 10:22 "And ye shall be hated of all men for My name's sake: but he that endureth to the end shall be saved."

5. Obedience: Obedience is an indicator of the true condition of the heart. The Bible makes a clear distinction between expressions of the mouth and expressions of the heart. Obedience is better than sacrifice.

Luke 6:46 "And why call ye me, Lord, Lord, and do not the things which I say?"

Titus 1:16 "They profess that they know God; but in works they deny Him, being abominable, and disobedient, and unto every good work reprobate."

Matthew 7:21-23
7:21 "Not every one that saith unto me, Lord, Lord, shall enter into the kingdom of heaven; but he that doeth the will of my Father which is in heaven."
7:22 "Many will say to Me in that day, Lord, Lord, have we not prophesied in thy name? And in thy name have cast out devils? And in thy name done many wonderful works?"
7:23 "And then I will profess unto them, I never knew you: depart from me, ye that work iniquity."

Acts 5:29 "Then Peter and the other apostles answered and said, We ought to obey God rather than men."

Revelation 22:14
22:14 "Blessed are they that do His commandments, that they may have right to the tree of life, and may enter in through the gates into the city"

Salvation is a condition of the heart. In other words, God is not interested in the flesh (body); He is interested in the heart because the heart motivates the workings of the body. God holds us responsible for the condition of our heart (repentance) even after we confess Jesus.

Salvation is based on more than just lip service and what we do matters more than what we say. For example, the biggest problem that people have with some politicians is that they will say whatever is necessary to get elected, but rarely follow through with their actions. In fact, charisma and charm will take you a long way with men, but God is not moved by charisma and carefully thought out speeches. Misleading motives and false intentions of the heart do not fool him.

Matthew 15:8 "This people draweth nigh unto me with their mouth, and honoureth me with their lips; but their heart is far from me."

Matthew 12:34-35
12:34 "O generation of vipers, how can ye, being evil, speak good things? For out of the abundance of the heart the mouth speaketh."
12:35 "A good man out of the good treasure of the heart bringeth forth good things: and an evil man out of the evil treasure bringeth forth evil things."

Luke 6:45 "A good man out of the good treasure of his heart bringeth forth that which is good; and an evil man out of the evil treasure of his heart bringeth forth that which is evil: for out of the abundance of the heart his mouth speaketh."

Matthew 23:28 "Even so ye also outwardly appear righteous unto men, but within ye are full of hypocrisy and iniquity."

Mark 7:6-7
7:6 "He answered and said unto them, Well hath Esaias prophesied of you hypocrites, as it is written, This people

honoureth me with their lips, but their heart is far from me."

7:7 "Howbeit in vain do they worship me, teaching for doctrines the commandments of men."

The Bible clearly warns us to judge a person by his fruits and not his mouth. This is very important for the church of today because deception and wolves in sheep's clothing face us at every turn.

Consider the following scripture:

John 6:44 "No man can come to Me, except the Father which hath sent me draw him: and I will raise him up at the last day"

The scripture above is referring to a condition of the heart and not a condition of the mouth. Salvation is about more than simply uttering a few words. The phrase "Jesus Christ, come into my life" is not a mystical phrase that can only be uttered by someone who means it. It is possible to say the phrase without being drawn by God and having no intentions of accepting Jesus Christ as Lord and Savior. It is also possible for a person to mean it when they say it but later decide to abandon their pledge due to the cares of this life. Some people simply determine being saved is too big a price to pay when it comes to forsaking the things of the world while others merely utter something they don't mean.

Revelation 3:9 "Behold, I will make them of the synagogue of satan, **which say** they are Jews, and are not, but do lie; behold, I will make them to come and worship before thy feet, and to know that I have loved thee."

Revelation 2:9 "I know thy works, and tribulation, and poverty, (but thou art rich) and I know the blasphemy of them **which say** they are Jews, and are not, but are the synagogue of satan.

II Corinthians 11:13-15
11:13 "For such are false apostles, deceitful workers, transforming themselves into the apostles of Christ."
11:14 "And no marvel; for Satan himself is transformed into an angel of light."
11:15 "Therefore it is no great thing if his ministers also be transformed as the ministers of righteousness; whose end shall be according to their works."

Consider the malefactors that were hanged on the cross next to Jesus. Both men asked to be saved but only one meant it from the heart. One wanted to be saved from death and the other sought salvation. The same remains true today. There are many reasons why people confess Jesus. Some seek Jesus for temporary refuge, some believe they will get a natural benefit in return, others want to be a part of something, some are deceivers seeking to spoil the church, and there are those that come because they genuinely seek to be with Jesus and follow His examples.

Luke 23:39-43
23:39 "And **one of the malefactors** which were hanged railed on Him, saying, If thou be Christ, **save thyself and us.** (*This man challenged Christ's authority and merely wanted to be saved from death, not to be with Christ*)
23:40 "**But the other** answering rebuked him, saying,

Dost not thou fear God, seeing thou art in the same condemnation?

23:41 And we indeed justly; for we receive the due reward of our deeds: *(heart of repentance)* but this man hath done nothing amiss. *(he recognized Christ for who He was)*

23:42 "And he said unto Jesus, Lord, remember me when thou comest into thy Kingdom. *(This man was not trying to escape death he wanted to be with Christ)*

23:43 "And Jesus said unto him, Verily I say unto thee, Today shalt thou be with me in paradise."

Both men wanted to be saved just in two very different ways. They each had their own motive for asking Jesus to save them. The first asked because he feared dying but the second malefactor asked from a heart of repentance. He acknowledged his sin and believed in the character of Jesus to grant Him life even after death.

Titus 2:11-14
2:11 "For the grace of God that bringeth salvation has appeared to all men,"

2:12 "Teaching us that, denying ungodliness and worldly lusts, we should live soberly, righteously, and Godly, in this present world."

2:13 "Looking for that blessed hope, and the glorious appearing of the great God and our Saviour Jesus Christ."

2:14 "Who gave Himself for us, that He might redeem us from all iniquity, and purify unto Himself a peculiar people, zealous of good works."

Acts 15:11 "But we believe that through the grace of the Lord Jesus Christ we shall be saved, even as they."

Consider this illustration:

A generous man (God) gives you a top of the line luxury car (salvation) out of the goodness of his heart. He tells you there is absolutely nothing you must do to merit the car other than receiving it. He then makes it known he has an unlimited supply of cars and will give them away to anyone that wants one (universal call). Next, he hands you the title, a set of keys, and an insurance policy paid in full, which he tells you can be used at any time.

Once the keys/title is in your hand, it is your responsibility to take care of the car if you expect to receive any benefit from it. If you refuse to put gas (the Word of God) in the car, it will not run very long. If you refuse to do the required maintenance (prayer), the car will not run very long, and if you neglect to secure the car (obedience), then the thief (satan) will come and steal the car. Even then you still have hope because you have an insurance policy (repentance), but it is your responsibility to call your agent (Jesus). Making the call retrieves your car and restores it to its original condition (a right heart). If you fail to make the call, then you will simply be out of a car (Salvation).

John 10:10 "The thief cometh not, but for to steal, and to kill, and to destroy: I am come that they might have life, and that they might have it more abundantly."

Given this scenario, why wouldn't a person make the call? Well, as strange as it may sound, a person may not make the call because there are so many other vehicles to drive he/she may choose to drive one of them. Another may say since it was free "easy come, easy go." Still others will conclude that taking care of a luxury vehicle is more trouble than it's worth, so good riddance. Last but not least, if the recipient refused to put gas in the car, refused to perform the required maintenance, and refused to secure the car then they probably could care less that the car is gone.

Salvation is a straight gate:

Matthew 7:13-14
7:13 "Enter ye in at the strait gate: for wide is the gate, and broad is the way, that leadeth to destruction, and many there be which go in thereat:
7:14 "Because strait is the gate, and narrow is the way, which leadeth unto life, and few there will be that find it."

Salvation is made possible through God's abundant grace:

Grace is the means by which we attain the perfect will of God. This grace is borne out of God's great love for man. It is immunity from our old nature and the gap between our imperfections and His perfection. The grace of God is sufficient to get us through our weakest moments, sustain us at our lowest point and gives us the strength to press forward. It is what draws men to repentance and is not a substitute for obedience to God's Word. The church must proclaim God's grace to the world.

II. Corinthians 12:9 "And He said unto me, My grace is sufficient for thee: for My strength is made perfect in weakness. Most gladly therefore will I rather glory in my infirmities, that the power of Christ may rest upon me."

Romans 3:24 "Being justified freely by His grace through the redemption that is in Christ Jesus"

II Timothy 2:1 "Thou therefore, my son, be strong in the grace that is in Christ Jesus"

Titus 2:11 "For the grace of God that bringeth salvation hath appeared to all men"

Ephesians 1:7 "In whom we have redemption through His blood, the forgiveness of sins, according to the riches of His grace"

Titus 3:5 "Not by works of righteousness which we have done, but according to His mercy He saved us, by the washing of regeneration and renewing of the Holy Ghost"

Romans 5:20 "Moreover the law entered, that the offense might abound. But where sin abounded, grace did much more abound"

Lamentations 3:22-23
3:22 "It is of the Lord's mercies that we are not consumed, because His compassions fail not"
3:23 "They are new every morning: great is thy faithfulness"

Micah 7:18 "Who is a God like unto thee, that pardoneth iniquity, and passeth by the transgression of the remnant of His heritage? He retaineth not His anger forever, because He delighteth in mercy"

Luke 1:50 "And His mercy is on them that fear Him from generation to generation"

Isaiah 55:7 "Let the wicked forsake his way, and the unrighteous man his thoughts: and let him return unto the Lord, and He will have mercy upon him; and to our God, for He will abundantly pardon"

Micah 7:18 "Who is a God like unto thee, that pardoneth iniquity, and passeth by the transgression of the remnant of His heritage? He retaineth not His anger forever, because He delighteth in mercy"

Hebrews 8:12 "For I will be merciful to their unrighteousness, and their sins and their iniquities will I remember no more"

Grace is a window into the heart of God. You don't have to work for grace, but there are things you must do to keep yourself under the realm of grace once you receive it. For instance, it is important to remember that God is holy and expects us to be holy. Grace means we are deemed holy in the eyes of God despite our shortcomings, sins, and weaknesses and we must continually strive to be holy. It is not a red carpet to willingly disobey God, live on both sides of the fence, and have our cake and eat it to.

Romans 5:1 "Therefore being justified by faith, we have peace with God through our Lord Jesus Christ."

Romans 5:15 "But not as the offense, so also is the free gift. For if through the offense of one many be dead, much more the grace of God, and the gift by grace, which is by one man, Jesus Christ, hath abounded unto many."

<u>Ephesians 2:8-9</u>
2:8 "For by grace are ye saved through faith; and that not of yourselves: it is the gift of God:"
2:9 "Not of works, lest any man should boast."

<u>Hebrews 4:16</u> "Let us therefore come boldly unto the throne of grace that we may obtain mercy, and find grace to help in time of need."

Chapter Six

Forgiveness and Repentance

The way of the Lord is paved with forgiveness and repentance. They are the essence of God's grace, but in order to benefit from their fruit you must believe you are entitled to them. Accept the fact that even though none of us deserved the pardon, nor could we afford to pay the price ourselves, Jesus paid the price of our ransom on the cross. You cannot earn forgiveness; you simply receive it and release it in the lives of others.

Ephesians 1:7 "In whom we have redemption through His blood, the forgiveness of sins according to the riches of His grace"

Forgiveness fosters an environment for change that is loving, supportive, and understanding. It is the essence of understanding the love of Jesus and how to walk in His character and is always available when we fall short. The Blood of Jesus is greater than sin and all our sins were nailed to the cross with Him.

Romans 3:23 "For all have sinned, and come short of the glory of God;"

The power of forgiveness is activated the moment

you make a decision to accept Jesus Christ as your Lord and Savior. It is a product of the finished work that was accomplished by Jesus Christ on the Cross. Good intentions do not cover sin, nor do they bring about God's justification whereby we are declared righteous in His eyes. Justification occurs when we accept the Blood sacrifice that was made by Jesus Christ on the cross. The power to wash away sins is in the Blood of Jesus.

God had a plan to redeem man from sin long before Jesus ever died on the Cross. In the Old Testament, before the Lord delivered the children of Israel out of Egypt, He instructed them to sacrifice a lamb and apply the blood on the two side posts and on the upper post of their houses. When judgment passed through the land of Egypt, it passed over every home where the blood was applied. Wherever the blood was not applied the first born of that house was killed by the plague (death) that passed through the land.

Judgment was not based upon the character or title of the individual but upon the blood that was applied to the doorpost. When death passed through the land, the only thing that stood in its way was the blood. Another point to consider is that those that were covered by the blood were safe as long as they stayed in the house where the blood was applied. If the first-born had left the home where the blood was applied, he would have suffered the same death as those that were not covered by the blood. This remains true today. Once you receive salvation, it is your responsibility to stay under the blood covering.

Exodus 12:5-7, 12-13
12:5 "Your lamb shall be without blemish, a male of the

first year: ye shall take it out from the sheep, or from the goats:"

12:6 "And ye shall keep it up until the fourteenth day of the same month: and the whole assembly of the congregation of Israel shall kill it in the evening"

12:7 "And they shall take of the blood, and strike it on the two side posts and on the upper door posts of the houses, wherein they shall eat."

12:12 "For I will pass through the land of Egypt this night, and will smite the firstborn in the land of Egypt, both man and beast; and against all the gods of Egypt I will execute judgment: I am the Lord."

12:13 "And the blood shall be to you for a token upon the houses where ye are: and when I see the blood, I will pass over you, and the plague shall not be upon you to destroy you, when I smite the land of Egypt."

This act of God foretold the redemptive work of the cross that would be accomplished through the blood of Jesus Christ, God's sacrificial lamb.

In the Day of Judgment, God will once again look for the blood covering to determine who shall be passed over because the end result of sin is death. The Bible states in Romans 3:23 "For all have sinned, and come short of the glory of God", but God through His grace and mercy has made the blood of Jesus available to cover us from judgment. God will look upon the blood instead of our sins. Salvation and forgiveness is all about the blood of Jesus.

Romans 5:12

5:12 "Wherefore, as by one man sin entered into the

world, and death by sin; and so death passed upon all men, for that all have sinned."

<u>Hebrews 9:22</u> "And almost all things are by the law purged with blood; and without shedding of blood is no remission"

<u>Hebrews 9:28</u> "So Christ was once offered to bear the sins of many; and unto them that look for Him shall He appear the second time without sin unto salvation

<u>Ephesians 1:7</u> "In whom we have redemption through His blood, the forgiveness of sins, according to the riches of His grace"

Forgiveness is not a substitute for accountability. To receive forgiveness means that I am not condemned for my past failures, my present shortcomings, offenses and misdeeds, whereas accountability ensures that there is an honest commitment to changing or correcting the behavior in the future. Accountability keeps us honest and is a good indicator of the true intentions of the heart. Corrective action is the steps that are taken to turn away from the offensive behavior or act. True repentance involves both corrective action and accountability.

<u>Romans 5:20</u> "Moreover the law entered, that the offense might abound. But where sin abounded, grace did much more abound"

Repentance is essential when seeking God's forgiveness, but it involves more than just words. It is a condition of the heart requiring examination and honesty accompanied by change. You must take an honest look at yourself and be willing to allow the Word of God to work on those areas of your life that are not lined up with His will. Too many people have adopted the belief that repentance is simply verbalizing the wrongs that they have committed.

<u>Matthew 15:8-9</u>
15:8 "This people draweth nigh unto me with their lips; but their heart is far from me."
15:9 "But in vain they do worship me, teaching for doctrines the commandments of men"

<u>Proverbs 28:13</u> "He that covereth his sins shall not prosper: but whoso **confesseth and forsaketh** them shall have mercy."

Many people have mastered the confession part of the Scripture but oftentimes neglect the turning away from the offensive behavior part.

<u>Luke 24:47</u>
24:47 "And that repentance and remission of sins should be preached in His name among all nations, beginning at Jerusalem."

<u>II Peter 3:9</u> "The Lord is not slack concerning His promise, as some men count slackness; but is longsuffering to us-ward, not willing that any should perish, but that all men should come to repentance."

The ministry of Jesus Christ was built on repentance and it is the essence of a relationship with Him. The way of the Lord must be paved through the message of repentance and turning away from sin. More and more this message is being lost out of fear that it may offend some people and because it does not draw large crowds like the messages concerning prosperity. There is nothing wrong with the messages concerning health and prosperity if they are preached in the context of a repented life that is lined up with the word of God, but what good are health and prosperity if you die in your sins? The Bible is flooded with promises of prosperity but those promises are conditioned upon obedience and being in right standing with God.

The potential danger that exists today is many people base their standing with God upon their outward success, and have become ignorant to the fact that Satan also has prosperity to give as he pleases. The same as God uses men to advertise His blessings the devil also uses men to create an illusion that you can be blessed without God. How can one envy something that they cannot see or desire something that does not appear to be within their reach? The Bible tells us that the love of money is the root of all evil so the devil works hard to get you to love money more than you love God. He merely grants riches to a select few and causes countless others to worship and emulate them. Some people are more concerned with what is going on in the lives of their favorite celebrity than they are about the things of God.

Jesus' ministry centered on repentance and his forerunner, John the Baptist, prepared His way through a message of repentance. The church must once again preach repentance in order to prepare the way for the glorious return of our Lord and savior Jesus Christ. The Lord seeks to find souls when He returns, not countless people driving Hummers and Cadillacs. This is not an indictment against wealth and nice rides because it is the will of God that His people be blessed.

I want to be clear that I do not subscribe to a beaten down, poverty mentality when it comes to the things of God. Just keep in mind that when He raptures the church the expensive cars are staying here and our prayer must be not to be left behind in them. Once again, God wants us to prosper and be in good health, but as a result of our obedience to Him. Prosperity should be the result of a life surrendered to Christ as opposed to being the focus. Prosperity without contentment is simply another form of lust.

Matthew 6:33 "But seek ye first the kingdom of God and His righteousness; and all these things shall be added unto you."

III. John 1:2
1:2 "Beloved, I wish above all things, that thou mayest prosper and be in health, even as thy soul prospereth."

John the Baptist "the forerunner of Christ" preached repentance.
Matthew 3:1-3
3:1 "In those days came John the Baptist, preaching in the wilderness of Judea,"
3:2 "And saying, Repent ye: for the kingdom of heaven is at hand."
3:3 "For this is he that was spoken of by the prophet Isaiah, saying, The voice of one crying in the wilderness, Prepare ye the way of the Lord, make His paths straight."

The Disciples of Christ preached repentance

Mark 6:12 "And they went out and preached that men should repent."

The ministry of Jesus Christ was built on repentance
Matthew 1:20-21

1:20 "But while he thought on these things, behold, the angel of the Lord appeared unto him in a dream, saying, Joseph, thou son of David, fear not to take unto thee Mary thy wife: for that which is conceived in her is of the Holy Ghost."

1:21 "And she shall bring forth a son, and thou shalt call His name JESUS: for He shall save His people from their sins."

Matthew 9:10-13

9:10 "And it came to pass, as Jesus sat at meat in the house, behold, many publicans and sinners came and sat down with Him and His disciples."

9:11 "And when the Pharisees saw it, they said unto His disciples, why eateth your Master with publicans and sinners?"

9:12 "But when Jesus heard that, he said unto them, They that be whole need not a physician, but they that are sick."

9:13 "But go ye and learn what that meaneth, I will have mercy, and not sacrifice: for I am not come to call the righteous, but sinners to repentance."

Luke 13:3 "I tell you, Nay: but, except ye repent, ye shall all likewise perish."

Matthew 4:17 "From that time Jesus began to preach, and to say, Repent: for the kingdom of heaven is at hand."

You can be prosperous and not repented. (Satan can also grant prosperity.)
Luke 4:5-7
4:5 "And the devil, taking him up into an high mountain, shewed unto him all the kingdoms of the world in a moment of time."

4:6 "And the devil said unto him, All this power will I give thee, and the glory of them: for that is delivered unto me; and to whomsoever I will I give it."

4:7 "If thou therefore wilt worship me, all shall be thine."

Prosperity without repentance is in vain.
Matthew 16:26 "For what is a man profited, if he shall gain the whole world, and lose his own soul? Or what shall a man give in exchange for his soul?

I Timothy 6:10 "For the love of money is the root of all evil: which while some have coveted after, they have erred from the faith, and pierced themselves through with many sorrows."

You must have the right motives.
John 6:26-27
6:26 "Jesus answered them and said, Verily, verily, I say unto you, Ye seek me, not because ye saw the miracles, but because ye did eat of the loaves, and were filled."

6:27 "Labour not for the meat which perisheth, but for that meat which endureth unto everlasting life, which the Son of Man shall give unto you: for Him hath God the Father sealed."

The key, as I stated earlier, is having the humility to look inward first and be honest. Acknowledge any shortcomings, failures, problems, issues, stumbling blocks, or hindrances in your life. Then seek the face of the Lord and ask for His forgiveness. Once you have repented, the door will be opened for true prosperity, healing and deliverance. The fact that sin got in is one thing (protect your mind, and guard your heart), but the bigger issue is allowing it to remain.

God, through Jesus Christ, has allowed us a way out of the condemnation and destruction of sin. You can't afford to allow sin to lie in your heart. Regardless of how many times you have messed up, you can call out on the blood of Jesus that was shed for your freedom. If your heart is right and sincere, then you will one day walk in your freedom. Oftentimes, the absence of a consistent prayer life, ungodly influences, or a lack of time spent in the Word is the primary cause of continuous stumbling.

II Corinthians 12:21 "And lest, when I come again, my God will humble me among you, and that I shall bewail many which have sinned already, and have not repented of the uncleanness and fornication and lasciviousness which they have committed"

I John 1:9 "If we confess our sins, He is faithful and just to forgive us our sins, and to cleanse us from all unrighteousness"

James 4:7 "Submit yourselves therefore to God. Resist the devil, and he will flee from you"

Isaiah 55:7 "Let the wicked forsake his way, and the unrighteous man his thoughts: and let him return unto the

Lord, and he will have mercy upon him: and to our God, for He will abundantly pardon"

<u>Matthew 8:9-10</u>
8:9 "When Jesus had lifted up Himself, and saw none but the woman, he said unto her, Woman, where are those thine accusers? Hath no man condemned thee?
8:10 "She said, No man, Lord. And Jesus said unto her, Neither do I condemn thee: go, and sin no more"

<u>John 5:14</u> "Afterward Jesus findeth him in the temple, and said unto him, Behold thou art made whole: sin no more, lest a worse thing come unto thee."

<u>Luke 19:10</u> "For the Son of Man is come to seek and to save that which was lost."

Be willing to forgive others:
Many people have a hard time forgiving themselves because they refuse to forgive others. Loving others gives you great insight into what it means to receive God's grace and mercy. When you grant forgiveness, you put yourself in a position to receive forgiveness. When you refuse to forgive, you become an agent of condemnation and guilt by disregarding the significance of the blood of Jesus and blocking its flow in the life of another. **Jesus paid the price so that all men could live free from the condemnation and guilt of sin.**

<u>Mark 11:25</u> "And when ye stand praying, forgive, if ye have ought against any: that your Father also which is in Heaven may forgive you your trespasses"

<u>Ephesians 4:32</u> "And be ye kind one to another, tender-

hearted, forgiving one another, even as God for Christ sake hath forgiven you"

Colossians 3:13 "Forbearing one another and forgiving one another, if any man have a quarrel against any: even as Christ forgave you, so also do ye"

Matthew 6:14 "For if ye forgive men their trespasses, your heavenly Father will also forgive you."

Luke 17:4 "And if he trespass against thee seven times in a day, and seven times in a day turn again to thee, saying, I repent; thou shall forgive him."

Matthew 18:21-22
18:21 "Then came Peter to Him, and said, Lord, how oft shall my brother sin against me, and I forgive him? till seven times?
18:22 "Jesus saith unto him, I say not unto thee, until seven times: but, until seventy times seven."

Once you're forgiven, quit carrying around the condemnation of sin because it prevents you from grasping God's vision for your life. You can't have hope in the future if you're haunted by your past. The devil can't stop a believer from obtaining the promises of God, but dwelling in the past can rob you of the precious faith needed to secure your entitlements to the future.

Condemnation, the mud of life, can slow you down, cause you to be stuck, or even to change course. The obstacles and shortcomings you faced in the past should not show up on the map to your future. Your future is attainable, free from condemnation, weights, and sin.

Romans 8:1 "There is therefore now no condemnation to them which are in Christ Jesus, who walk not after the flesh, but after the Spirit"

Isaiah 43:25 "I even I, am He that blotteth out thy transgressions for mine own sake, and will not remember thy sins"

Ezekiel 18:21 "But if the wicked will turn from all his sins that he hath committed, and keep all my statutes, and do that which is lawful and right, he shall surely live, he shall not die"

Ephesians 1:7 "In whom we have redemption through His blood, the forgiveness of sins, according to the riches of His grace"

Acts 2:38 "Then Peter said unto them, Repent, and be baptized every one of you in the name of Jesus Christ for the remission of sins, and ye shall receive the gift of the Holy Ghost"

Luke 15:7 "I say unto you, that likewise joy shall be in Heaven over one sinner that repenteth, more than ninety and nine just persons, which need no repentance"

Psalm 34:18 "The Lord is nigh unto them that are of a broken heart; and saveth such as be of a contrite spirit"

Acts 8:22 "Repent therefore of this thy wickedness, and pray God, if perhaps the thoughts of thine heart may be forgiven thee"

Acts 3:19 "Repent ye therefore, and be converted, that your sins may be blotted when the times of refreshing shall come from the presence of the Lord"

Matthew 3:2 "And saying, Repent ye: for the kingdom of Heaven is at hand"

Luke 13:3 "I tell you, Nay: but, except ye repent, ye shall all likewise perish"

The Bible is very clear that repentance is connected to salvation. In fact, Jesus Christ Himself drives this point home in the letters to the seven churches contained in the book of Revelation. Within the letters, the Lord addresses the churches concerning various compromising states that He finds them in that require repentance. When the Lord returns, He is looking for a church without spot and blemish. Remember, His ministry was built on repentance and the church was given the charge to continue in His ministry. The warnings contained in the letters illustrate salvation is not a license to sin, and the church is faced with a decision to either repent and serve Christ, or face eternal separation. The following letters were written to the church of today as a warning to repent before His glorious return. The following is a snapshot to illustrate the fact that the message of repentance is applicable even after you get saved. I must alert the reader that there is much more to know and understand concerning the messages than is discussed here. This is only a snapshot.

Church #1 The active church, sound in doctrine, but deficient in love.
Revelation 2:1-5

2:1 "Unto the angel of the church of Ephesus write; These things saith He that holdeth the seven stars in His right hand, who walketh in the midst of the seven golden candlesticks;"

2:2 "I know thy works, and thy labor, and thy patience, and how thou canst not bear them which are evil: and thou hast tried them which say they are apostles, and are not, and hast found them liars:"

2:3 "And hast borne, and hast patience, and for my names sake hast labored, and hast not fainted."

2:4 "Nevertheless I have somewhat against thee, because thou hast left thy first love."

2:5 "Remember therefore from whence thou art fallen, and repent, and do the first works; or else I will come quickly, and will remove thy candlestick out of His place, except thou repent."

Each of the seven churches discussed is represented by a candlestick which designates the church's position in the body of Christ. He warns this church to repent or else He would remove their candlestick out of its place. The Lord instructs them to do their first works and return back to Him.

Like many saints in the church today, they have forgotten about the true essence and purpose of salvation, which is to share the love of Jesus with others. . The passion and love they once had for Jesus dissipated over time and they have become indifferent simply going through the motions. Although they labor in Christ, they have backed away from some of their first works and zeal they once shared in Christ because their love has grown cold. They no longer share the excitement they had when they first got saved and their prayer lives are probably standardized at best. The Lord is giving them space to repent and recapture the love and excitement they once shared in Him.

Church #2 The poor but rich church.
<u>Revelation 2:8-11</u>

2:8 "And unto the angel of the church in Smyrna write; These things saith the first and the last which was dead, and is alive;"

2:9 "I know thy works, and tribulation, and poverty, (but thou art rich) and I know the blasphemy of them which say they are Jews, and are not, but are the synagogue of Sa'tan.

2:10 "Fear none of these things which thou shalt suffer: behold, the devil shall cast some of you into prison, that ye may be tried; and ye shall have tribulation ten days: be thou faithful unto death, and I will give thee a crown of life."

2:11 "He that hath an ear, let him hear what the Spirit saith unto the churches; He that overcometh shall not be hurt of the second death."

The Lord knows the lives of the saints; those that have good works and the blasphemy of those that call themselves saints but make a false profession. We find that endurance is connected to salvation. The second death describes eternal separation from God and the Lord states that "he that overcomes shall not be hurt of the second death." The notion of being an over-comer is tied to being steadfast and having the faith to hold onto your profession of Jesus Christ until the very end. There will be those that leave the faith in the face of danger, persecution, worldly ambition, and other stumbling blocks that Satan will place in their way, but the Lord is faithful and has equipped us with everything we need to overcome. We can choose to believe God until the end or succumb to the pressures of the world.

Revelation 21:7-8
21:7 "He that overcometh shall inherit all things; and I will be his God, and he shall be my son."
21:8 "But the fearful, and unbelieving, and the abominable, and murderers, and whoremongers, and sorcerers, and idolaters, and all liars, shall have their part in the lake which burneth with fire and brimstone: which is the second death."

Church # 3 The heretical church
Revelation 2:12-16
2:12 "And to the angel of the church in Pergamos write; These things saith He which hath the sword with two edges;"
2:13 "I know thy works, and where thou dwellest, even where Satan's seat is: and thou holdest fast my name, and hast not denied my faith, even in those days wherein Anti-pas was my faithful martyr, who was slain among you, where Satan dwelleth."
2:14 "But I have a few things against thee, because thou hast there them that hold the doctrine of Balaam, who taught Balac to cast a stumbling block before the children of Israel, to eat things sacrificed unto idols, and to commit fornication."
2:15 "So hast thou also them that hold the doctrine of the Nicolaitanes, which thing I hate."
2:16 "Repent; or else I will come unto thee quickly, and will fight against them with the sword of my mouth.'

Here the Lord reproves the church for evil associations and false doctrine is condemned. He also admonishes the church for sin and addresses the issue of fornication. The Lord warns the church to repent or else He would come upon them suddenly and fight against them with the sword of His mouth (His word).

Once again it's important to remember that Jesus is addressing the church, not the world. The point is grace is not a rocking chair and it is imperative that the church continue to walk in its true calling and not become complacent in sin.

Church #4 The church of the false prophetess
Revelation 2:18-26

2:18 "And unto the angel of the church in Thyatira write; These things saith the Son of God, who hath His eyes like unto a flame of fire, and His feet are like fine brass;"

2:19 "I know thy works, and charity, and service, and faith, and thy patience, and thy works; and the last to be more than the first."

2:20 "Notwithstanding I have a few things against thee, because thou sufferest that woman Jezebel, which calleth herself a prophetess, to teach and to seduce my servants to commit fornication, and to eat things sacrificed unto idols."

2:21 "And I gave her space to repent of her fornication; and she repented not."

2:22 "Behold, I will cast her into a bed, and them that commit adultery with her into great tribulation, except they repent of their deeds."

2:23 "And I will kill her children with death; and all the churches shall know that I am He which searcheth the reins and the hearts: and I will give unto every one of you according to your works."

2:24 "But unto you I say, and the rest in Thyatira, as many as have not this doctrine, and which have not known the depths of Satan, as they speak; I will put upon you none other burden."

2:25 "But that which ye have already hold fast till I come."

2:26 "And he that overcometh, and keepeth my works unto the end, to him will I give power over the nations."

Jesus is a searcher of the hearts and addresses the church concerning evil associations, false prophets, and the defilement of sin. He specifically addresses the issue of spiritual adultery spawned by the sexual immorality prevalent in this church. He states that this church was given space to repent but refused, and warns them their sins would be judged, and of the subsequent consequences that would follow. We must be very watchful when it comes to sexual sins. There are those that are engaging in fornication, shacking, adultery, and other forms of lust and sexual sins that must be set free. The Lord urges the church to remain faithful and hold fast to that which is good until He comes. In verse 2:26, the Lord again instructs the church to resist temptation and follow after His examples.

The church must continue to take a stand against those things contrary to the Word of God despite what societal trends may be. We live in a world that has increasingly adopted a free-willed attitude concerning fornication and adultery and its influence will continue to extend into the church. Too many people have become comfortable living in sin and shouting on Sunday. The unadulterated gospel is the only thing separating those practicing sin from the judgment of God.

Church #5 The dying church
Revelation 3:1-5

3:1 "And unto the angel of the church in Sardis write; These things saith He that hath the seven Spirits of God, and the seven stars; I know thy works, and that thou hast a name that thou livest, and art dead."

3:2 "Be watchful, and strengthen the things that are ready to die: for I have not found thy works perfect before God."

3:3 "Remember therefore how thou hast received and heard, and hold fast, and repent. If therefore thou shalt not watch, I will come as thief, and thou shalt not know what hour I will come upon thee."

3:4 "Thou hast a few names in Sardis which have not defiled their garments; and they shall walk with me in white: for they are worthy."

3:5 "He that overcometh, the same shall be clothed in white raiment; and I will not blot out his name out of the book of life, but I will confess his name before my Father, and before His angels."

Here the Lord reproves the church concerning formalism and its half-heartedness, and professes it is dead in sin. Although they go through the motions of gathering together each week, this church lacks any power to effect change. This may be a church stagnated by tradition and man-made doctrine to the point that it restricts a fresh move of the Holy Spirit. He warns the church He will come as a thief in the night, verse 3:3, and states that He that does not overcome will not be confessed before the

Father, verse 3:5, and his name shall be blotted out of the book of life.

Revelation 20:15 "And whosoever was not found written in the book of Life was cast into the lake of fire."

Three key points to consider:
1. Jesus is addressing the church not the world
2. Whose names are contained in the book of life that He threatens to blot out and not confess before the Father.
3. When Jesus states that He will come as a thief in the night, what does this mean?

Jesus is addressing the church not the world:
The first point illustrates the church is still held accountable for its works. The Lord urges the church to repent which tells us there is a way of escape, but He also speaks of judgment for those that choose not to repent. We are still held accountable for our works so it is possible for a person to have once confessed Christ, but over time make a decision to abandon the things of God.

Whose names are contained in the book of life that He threatens to blot out and not confess before the Father?
Exodus 32:33 "And the Lord said unto Moses, Whosoever hath sinned against me, him will I blot out of my book."

Psalm 69:28 "Let them be blotted out of the book of the living, and not be written with the righteous."

Luke 10:20 "Notwithstanding in this rejoice, not that

the spirits are subject unto you; but rather rejoice, because your names are written in Heaven."

Hebrews 12:23 "To the general assembly and church of the firstborn, which are written in heaven, and to God the judge of all, and to the spirits of just men made perfect."

Philippians 4:3 "And I entreat thee also, true yokefellow, help those women which labored with me in the gospel, with Clement also, and with other my fellow laborers, whose names are in the book of life."

Revelation 20:12 "And I saw the dead, small and great, stand before God; and the books were opened: and another book was opened, which is the book of life: and the dead were judged out of those things which were written in the book, according to their works."

Revelation 21:27 "And there shall in no wise enter into it any thing that defileth, neither whatsoever worketh abomination, or maketh a lie: but they which are written in the Lamb's book of life."

Revelation 22:19 "And if any man shall take away from the words of the book of this prophecy, God shall take away his part out of the book of life, and out of the holy city, and from the things which are written in this book."

The book of life contains the names of the Saints of God. Those whose names are found in the Book of Life shall be eternally connected to God and shall not be hurt by the second death. Those not written in the Book of Life shall experience the second death, which is eternal separation from God.

When Jesus states that He will come as a thief in the night what does this mean?

One way the word thief is used in the New Testament is to describe the suddenness of Jesus coming, the state of unreadiness and the lack of watchfulness for those that shall not escape. He does not address His own as a thief (children of the light), nor does He state His coming would catch them unaware. He addresses the world (children of darkness) as a thief in the same manner He warns us Satan is a thief. Those in fellowship with Jesus can see the writing on the wall. They can sense the time because of the Spirit within them and are gravitating even closer to the things of God, but those in the world lie in darkness. The Bible instructs us to be watchful so that day does not take us unaware as a thief in the night.

<u>I Thessalonians 5:1-9</u>

5:1 "But of the times and the seasons, brethren, ye have no need that I write unto you."

5:2 "For yourselves know perfectly that the day of the Lord so cometh as a thief in the night."

5:3 "For when they say, Peace and safety; then sudden destruction cometh upon them, as travail upon a woman with child; and they shall not escape."

5:4 "But ye, brethren, are not in darkness, that that day should overtake you as a thief."

5:5 "Ye are the children of light, and the children of the day: we are not of the night, nor of darkness."

5:6 "Therefore let us not sleep, as do others; but let us watch and be sober."

5:7 "For they that sleep sleep in the night; and they that be drunken are drunken in the night."

5:8 "But let us, who are of the day, be sober, putting

on the breastplate of faith and love; and for an helmet, the hope of salvation."

5:9 "For God hath not appointed us to wrath, but to obtain salvation by our Lord Jesus Christ."

Matthew 24:42-44

24:42 "Watch therefore: for ye know not what hour your Lord doth come."

24:43 "But know this, that if the Goodman of the house had known in what watch the thief would come, he would have watched, and would not have suffered his house to be broken up."

24:44 "Therefore be ye also ready: for in such an hour ye think not the Son of man cometh."

Mark 13:34-37

13:34 "For the Son of man is as a man taking a far journey, who left his house, and gave authority to his servants, and to every man his work, and commanded the porter to watch."

13:35 "Watch ye therefore: for ye know not when the master of the house cometh, at even, or at midnight, or at the cockcrowing, or in the morning."

13:36 "Lest coming suddenly he find you sleeping."

13:37 "And what I say unto you I say unto all, Watch."

Luke 21:34-36

21:34 "And take heed to yourselves, lest at any time your hearts be overcharged with surfeiting and drunkenness, and cares of this life, and so that day come upon you unawares."

21:35 "For as a snare shall it come upon all them that dwell on the face of the whole earth."

21:36 "Watch ye therefore, and pray always, that ye may be accounted worthy to escape all these things that shall come to pass, and to stand before the Son of Man."

<u>II Peter 3:8-10</u>
3:8 "But, beloved, be not ignorant of this one thing, that one day is with the Lord as a thousand years, and a thousand years as one day."

3:9 "The Lord is not slack concerning His promise, as some men count slackness; but is longsuffering to us-ward, not willing that any should perish, but that all should come to repentance."

3:10 "But the day of the Lord will come as a thief in the night; in the which the heavens shall pass away with a great noise, and the elements shall melt with fervent heat, the earth also and the works that are therein shall be burned up."

6 The loyal church
<u>Revelation 3:6-11</u>
3:6 "He that hath an ear, let him hear what the Spirit saith unto the churches."

3:7 "And to the angel of the church in Philadelphia write; These things saith He that is holy, He that is true, He that hath the key of David, He that openeth, and no man shutteth; and shutteth, and no man openeth."

3:8 "I know thy works: behold, I have set before thee an open door, and no man can shut it: for thou hast a little strength, and hast kept my word, and hast not denied my name."

3:9 "Behold, I will make them of the synagogue of satan, which say they are Jews, and are not, but do lie; behold, I will make them to come and worship before thy feet, and to know that I have loved thee."

3:10 "Because thou hast kept the word of my patience, I also will keep thee from the hour of temptation, which shall come upon all the world, to try them that dwell upon the earth."

3:11 "Behold, I come quickly: hold fast which thou hast, that no man take thy crown."

Jesus states in verse 3:8 that this church has "kept my word" and hast not "denied my name," and again in verse 3:10 He states, "thou hast kept the word of my patience." As a result, He states, "I will keep thee from the hour of temptation which shall come upon all the world, to try them that dwell upon the earth." This church is described as the loyal church; they remained faithful until the end. The Lord states He will exalt the true believers and abase those that make a false profession.

It is important to understand the attributes of this church. This church made a decision to keep the words of the Lord and as a result the Lord keeps them. This supports the confidence we have in the word of God keeping us. You can be kept and assured of your salvation if you make a choice to follow the instructions given to us by our Lord and Savior Jesus Christ. The correct phrase should be "once saved, always saved if I make a decision to keep Jesus first in my life."

#7 The Lukewarm, Self-Satisfied, Church
<u>Revelation 3:14-19</u>

3:14 "And unto the angel of the church of the La-od-o-ceans, write; These things saith the A-men, the faithful and true witness, the beginning of the creation of God;"

3:15 "I know thy works, that thou art neither cold nor hot: I would thou wert cold or hot."

3:16 "So then because thou art lukewarm, and neither cold nor hot, I will spue thee out of my mouth."

3:17 "Because thou sayest, I am rich, and increased with goods, and have need of nothing; and knowest not that thou are wretched, and miserable, and poor, and blind, and naked:"

3:18 "I counsel thee to buy of me gold tried in the fire, that thou mayest be rich; and white raiment that thou mayest be clothed, and that the shame of thy nakedness do not appear; and anoint thine eyes with eye salve, that thou mayest see."

3:19 "As many as I love, I rebuke and chasten: be zealous therefore, and repent."

This church is admonished for self-righteousness, formalism, back sliding, indifference, and half-heartedness. In verse 3:16 the Lord warns that He will "spew them out of His mouth" and urges them to repent in verse 3:19. This church is indecisive and lacks action. They are deceived, complacent, and have become powerless in the fight to win souls to Jesus. This church is devoid of fire and boldness in the faith and is in danger of becoming spiritually destitute. The Lord counsels them to repent out of the great love He has for them. He chastens them to discover the true riches of a precious life rooted in Christ and has given them space to repent and get things right before He returns.

The underlying message given to the churches is to repent. The Lord knows the heart of His people and is displeased with the sin prevalent in the church today. Although we have mastered the ceremony, there are those that simply make a show for men. They are proficient at describing holiness but live a life of sin and deception once they leave the building. The more watered down the church becomes the more prevalent this hypocrisy. The Lord is warning His people to fight against this spirit.

The good news is that where sin abounds there is always more grace. Grace is available to the individual that exercises his/her right to receive it through repentance. Each individual that demonstrates the characteristics described above is given a choice to either repent or ignore the warnings given by the Lord and refuse to change course. The consequences of ignoring the warnings is that individual will be a good candidate to hear the words "depart from me ye that work iniquity, I never knew you."

Chapter Seven

Obedience is Essential

<u>Romans 10:2-3</u>
10:2 "For I bear them record that they have a zeal of God, but not according to knowledge."
10:3 "For they being ignorant of God's righteousness, and going about to establish their own righteousness, have not submitted themselves unto the righteousness of God."

In order for the church to prepare the way of the Lord, we must practice obedience to the Word of God. Obedience, an act of humility and reverence, is essential to membership in God's family. It is a sign of your love and trust the same way disobedience is a sign of arrogance and rebellion. To say you trust God, but fail to do the things He has instructed you to do is a contradiction.

<u>I Samuel 15:22</u> "And Samuel said, Hath the Lord as great delight in burnt offerings and sacrifices, as in obeying the voice of the Lord? Behold, to obey is better than sacrifice, and to hearken than the fat of rams."

To follow God is to abandon your will even in the face of sacrifice. It requires a surrendered heart and a willing mind, and is essential to salvation. Many times obedience means you will not be in the 'in crowd' or win public opinion. That is ok. The Bible says obedience sets apart those that truly love the Lord and are members of His family.

Being obedient doesn't mean you will not make mistakes or sometimes miss the mark when it comes to living a life pleasing to God; rather it means you have made a commitment to obey the will of God to the best of your ability. Coupled in the act of striving for the will of God is a heart of repentance. Your love for God convicts you when you miss the mark and you strive to make it right or correct the wrong.

Matthew 12:50 "For whosoever shall do the will of my Father which is in heaven, the same is my brother, and sister, and mother."

Luke 8:21 "And He answered and said unto them, My mother and my brethren are these which hear the word of God, and do it"

John 14:23 "Jesus answered and said unto him, If a man love Me, he will keep My words: and my Father will love him, and we will come unto him, and make our abode with him."

John 15:10 "If ye keep my commandments, ye shall abide in my love; even as I have kept my Father's commandments, and abide in His love."

John 14:21 "He that hath my commandments, and keepeth them, he it is that loveth me: and he that loveth me shall be loved of my Father, and I will love him, and will manifest myself to him."

John 15:14 "Ye are my friends, if ye do whatsoever I command you."

John 15:17 "These things I command you, that ye love one another."

Luke 6:46 "And why call ye me, Lord, Lord, and do not the things which I say?"

Luke 11:28 "But he said, Yea rather, blessed are they that hear the word of God, and keep it."

Obedience requires us to make a firm decision. You cannot straddle the fence nor be neutral and expect to live saved. There is no middle ground when it comes to the things of God. You are either with Him or against Him. Too many people, including some in the church, are deceived into thinking God will accept them despite the choices that they make. The Bible says you can come to God as you are, but doesn't state you are supposed to stay that way. In fact, the Bible states in II Corinthians 5:17 "Therefore if any man be in Christ, he is a new creature: old things are passed away; behold, all things are become new." Becoming a new creature is contingent upon obedience to the word of God. The more you line up with the word, the more you let go of your old nature and old ways of thinking.

I Corinthians 10:21 "You cannot drink the cup of the Lord, and the cup of devils: ye cannot be partakers of the Lord's table, and the table of devils."

Romans 1:18 "For the wrath of God is revealed from heaven against all ungodliness and unrighteousness of men, who hold the truth in unrighteousness."

I. John 2:3-6
2:3 "And hereby we do know that we know Him, if we keep His commandments."
2:4 "He that saith, I know Him, and keepeth not His commandments, is a liar, and the truth is not in him."
2:5 "But whoso keepeth His word, in him verily is the love of God perfected: hereby know we that we are in Him."
2:6 "He that saith he abideth in Him ought himself also so to walk, even as He walked."

Words alone are not a cloak from God's judgment of ungodliness. Because I asked the Lord into my life seven years ago doesn't mean I now have immunity to willingly and continually engage in sin and still escape the judgment of God. God expects us to be obedient but when we fall short, He expects us to repent and turn away from the offensive behavior. Repentance through the blood of Jesus is God's immunity from sin and judgment. If you choose not to repent and live like a devil, then you shall be judged as a devil.

Revelations 22:11 "He that is unjust, let him be unjust still: and he which is filthy, let him be filthy still: and he that is righteous, let him be righteous still: and he that is holy, let him be holy still."

I Peter 4:17-18
4:17 "For the time is come that judgment must begin at the house of God: and if it first begin at us, what shall the end be of them that obey not the gospel of God?"
4:18 "And if the righteous scarcely be saved, where shall the ungodly and the sinner appear?"

II Peter 2:9 "The Lord knoweth how to deliver the Godly out of temptations, and to reserve the unjust unto the day of judgment to be punished."

II Peter 3:7 "But the heavens and the earth, which are now, by the same word are kept in store, reserved unto fire against the day of judgment and perdition of ungodly men."

Ephesians 5:5-6
5:5 "For this ye know, that no whoremonger, nor unclean person, nor covetous man, who is an idolater, hath any inheritance in the kingdom of Christ and of God."
5:6 "Let no man deceive you with vain words: for because of these things cometh the wrath of God upon the children of disobedience."

Jude 1:14-15
1:14 "And Enoch also, the seventh from Adam, prophesied of these, saying, Behold, the Lord cometh with ten thousands of His saints."
1:15 "To execute judgment upon all, and to convince all that are ungodly among them of all their ungodly deeds which they have ungodly committed, and of all their hard speeches which ungodly sinners have spoken against Him."

Disobedience is a form of neglect or taking the grace of God for granted. When we try to pull God down to our standards as opposed to striving to obey His Word, we lose reverence for God and water down His commandments. Because He is holy, He wants us to be holy. For example, God's standard says fornication is a sin, whereas; the standard of the world says fornication is ok because God is my homeboy and He knows my heart. The more comfortable we get with God according to worldly standards, the more we lose the fear of God and the notion of consequences.

Proverbs 111:10 "The fear of the Lord is the beginning of wisdom: a good understanding have all they that do His commandments: his praise endureth for ever."

God is indeed our best friend, our comforter, and our protector to name a few, but He is still God. Titles carry meaning and respect and people should be mindful of this when they refer to Jesus Christ as their homeboy. Some will argue this is extreme or even fanaticism, but ask yourself—has morality gotten better or worst with society's watered down version of religion? I think it would be easy for any honest person to conclude that the more we attempt to make God our drinking buddy the more society strays away from His commandments. It is no different than parents that choose to be pals with their children as opposed to parents. Instead of being addressed as Mom and Dad, the children simply refer to them as Jan and Jim.

We cannot neglect the grace and mercy of God by actively engaging in sin and hiding behind phrases such as: "I have my own relationship with God." You may have your own relationship with your homeboy, but the Word of God had better define your relationship with Him.

The more we neglect the will of God through disobedience, the more we become numb to the judgment of God. We have become a society of men that have lost our fear of God, blind and accepting of the reasoning of the ignorant. We are becoming a people who will believe anything that sounds good and accept anything everybody else believes. It has become almost comical when we see certain celebrities that willingly practice and promote sin and then thank their Lord and Savior Jesus Christ for making it all possible. I say almost comical because countless young people embrace these same individuals as role models, and adopt the same standard in their own lives when it comes to the things of God. They are left with the impression that as long as they acknowledge God when they're sinning they have immunity from judgment. Not only are many in the spotlight guilty of this, but also every Christian that condones the same hypocrisy. This is not to say that these people aren't good people. They are just not godly people. The Lord is not pleased and it is time for us to repent.

Hebrews 2:2-3
2:2 "For if the word spoken by angels was steadfast, and every transgression and disobedience received a just recompense of reward;"
2:3 "How shall we escape, if we neglect so great salvation; which at first began to be spoken by the Lord, and was confirmed unto us by them that heard Him."

As I stated earlier, being obedient requires making a decision to be totally committed. It is a commitment to be available for God's purpose and a willingness to abandon our own, a pledge to actively pursue the things of God and learn more and more about His ways; it is making the most of every opportunity and using our talents and resources in ways that glorify Him.

We become prisoners of Christ by choice and volunteer our lives as a witness to His delivering power. We are walking billboards advertising His many blessings, abundant grace and mercy, enduring challenges and giving others hope, and always ready to testify and set the record straight concerning His goodness. Our lives are the stories others read as we demonstrate the Word of God through the manner in which we live. By adopting His character and abandoning our own, we joyfully sacrifice our way of thinking while praising Him for His love and goodness.

Romans 12:1 "I beseech you therefore, brethren, by the mercies of God, that ye present your bodies a living sacrifice, holy acceptable unto God, which is your reasonable service."

I John 2:3 "And hereby we do know that we know Him, if we keep His commandments"

Chapter Eight

Works Matter

It has already been established that salvation is not received through works; rather it is a free gift from God. Once again I strongly stand on what the word says in regards to God's unmerited gift of the blood of Jesus Christ. You do not have to work to receive salvation.

Even though salvation is received without works, your works are still important once you are saved. God judges the heart and the outward manifestation, works, is a good indicator of what is really going on in your heart. Works not only allow others to see where you stand in relationship to God, but also play a key role in self examination. If you say you love Jesus but manifest the ways of the world then you need to get your heart right with God. Whatever is in your heart will determine what your works are.

I John 3:19-21
3:19 "And hereby we know that we are of the truth, and shall assure our hearts before Him."
3:20 "For if our heart condemn us, God is greater than our heart, and knoweth all things."
3:21 "Beloved, if our heart condemn us not, then we have confidence toward God."

It is also important to point out that not all the references to works have to do with lifestyle choices. There are also works that deal with productivity (service) in the Kingdom, and there is a distinction made between the two. The works dealing with lifestyle choices (obedience) impact personal salvation, whereas the works that deal with productivity are connected to heavenly privileges (rewards), and the loss suffered for a lack thereof.

Psalm 62:12 "Also unto thee, O Lord, belongeth mercy: for thou renderest to every man according to his work."

Matthew 16:27 "For the Son of Man shall come in the glory of His father with His angels; and then He shall reward every man according to his works."

Revelation 22:12 "And, behold, I come quickly; and my reward is with me, to give every man according as his work shall be."

I Corinthians 3:13-15
3:13 "Every man's work shall be made manifest: for the day shall declare it, because it shall be revealed by fire; and the fire shall try every man's work of what sort it is."
3:14 "If any man's work abide which he hath built thereupon, he shall receive a reward."
3:15 "If any man's work shall be burned, he shall suffer loss: but he himself shall be saved; yet so as by fire."

The reference to fire used in verse 3:13 is not referring to hell fire. This reference to fire describes God's refining process similar to how gold is refined. Consider the following verses:

I Peter 1:7 "That the trial of your faith, being much more precious than of gold that perisheth, though it be tried with fire, might be found unto praise and honour and glory at the appearing of Jesus Christ."

Matthew 13:41-42
13:41 "The Son of Man shall send forth His angels, and they shall gather out of His kingdom all things that offend, and them which do iniquity;"
13:42 "And shall cast them into a furnace of fire: there shall be wailing and gnashing of teeth."

We see that there are two different types of fires being described because we know there will be no weeping and gnashing of teeth in heaven.

The following illustration may help to shed more light on this subject:

An employer has three employees and each one is evaluated as to how well he performs his particular assignment and rewarded accordingly.

Employee one comes to work late each day, is too lazy to study his craft, fails to refine or improve his skills, and has a very hard time staying focused on his assignments. Oftentimes, he hinders his co-workers' productivity because his assignments are usually incomplete or don't get done at all. The employer is very disappointed at the employee's lack of focus and responsibility and speaks to him about it. When made aware of his shortcomings, the employee apologizes for his lack of service and makes a commitment to do better. Because he shows up for work everyday, acknowledges his shortcomings, and apologizes for his faults, the employer allows him to keep his job.

This represents the individual whose works will be burnt up when tried in the fire but he will still be saved. Although he is not expanding the Kingdom, he is still in fellowship with God and repents for his shortcomings. He will make it into heaven but will have no rewards or crowns to lie at the Lord's feet.

Employee number two shows up on time everyday, continues to improve his skills, is successful in his assignments, acknowledges his mistakes, and makes his fellow workers better people because of his leadership.

The employer is so pleased with his success he sends him to recruit more workers to the company. The employer even gives him a promotion and a raise to reward his faithfulness.

This represents the individual whose works will be more precious than gold when tried in the fire. He will not only make it into heaven but will also have crowns to lie before the Lord's feet. He will enjoy earthly rewards and heavenly ones as well.

The last employee refuses to abide by the company rules and only shows up for work when it is convenient for him. His employer, on several occasions, has warned him concerning his behavior, but he refuses to acknowledge his wrongdoing and continues to violate company rules and procedures.

The employer, a very compassionate man, has no choice but to either fire him or change the rules to accommodate him. Knowing he cannot change the rules of the company to accommodate the disobedient employee, he goes to him again and again to request his compliance. Seeing the employee refuses to comply, he has no choice but to fire him.

This represents the individual that has made a decision

to ignore the will of God and whose heart has become cold and hardened. He will suffer the consequences of his choice which is eternal separation from God (hell fire). The point is God did not decide the fate of this individual. He chose his own fate through his disobedience.

More scriptures on how works, the heart, and salvation are related:

Jeremiah 17:9-10

17:9 "The heart is deceitful above all things, and desperately wicked: who can know it?"

17:10 "I the Lord search the heart, I try the reins, even to give every man according to his ways, and according to the fruit of his doings."

Romans 2:3-11

2:3 "And thinkest thou this, O man, that judgest them which do such things, and doest the same, that thou shalt escape the judgment of God?"

2:4 "Or despisest thou the riches of His goodness and forbearance and longsuffering; not knowing that the goodness of God leadeth thee to repentance."

2:5 "But after thy hardness and impenitent heart treasurest up unto thyself wrath against the day of wrath and revelation of the righteous judgment of God."

2:6 "Who will render to every man according to his deeds."

2:7 "To them who by patient continuance in well doing seek for glory and honour and immortality, eternal life."

2:8 "But unto them who are contentious, and do not obey the truth, but obey unrighteousness, indignation and wrath,"

2:9 "Tribulation and anguish upon every soul of man that doeth evil, of the Jew first, and also of the Gentile."

2:10 "But glory, honour, and peace, to every man that worketh good, to the Jew first, and also to the Gentile."

2:11 "For there is no respect of persons with God."

II. Corinthians 5:10 "For we must all appear before the judgment seat of Christ; that every one may receive the things done in his body, according to that he hath done, whether it be good or bad."

James 2:14-20

2:14 "What doth it profit, my brethren, though a man say he hath faith, and have not works? Can faith save him?"

2:15 "If a brother or sister be naked, and destitute of daily food,"

2:16 "And one of you say unto them, Depart in peace, be ye warmed and filled; notwithstanding ye give them not those things which are needful to the body; what doth it profit?"

2:17 "Even so faith, if it hath not works, is dead, being alone."

2:18 "Yea, a man may say, Thou hast faith, and I have works: shew me thy faith without thy works, and I will shew thee my faith by my works."

2:19 "Thou believest that there is one God; thou doest well: the devils also believe, and tremble."

2:20 "But wilt thou know, O vain man, that faith without works is dead?"

I Peter 1:15-17

1:15 "But as He which hath called you is holy, so be ye holy in all manner of conversation."

1:16 "Because it is written, Be ye holy; for I am holy."

1:17 "And if ye call on the Father, who without respect

of persons judgeth according to every man's work, pass the time of your sojourning here in fear:"

Once again, you do not have to work your way into Heaven because the work has already been completed! There is nothing you can do to merit heaven. You simply must have a heart to receive the gift. Where there is sin, there is always more grace, but grace is not a license to sin.

Your works are a good indicator as to the true condition of your heart and a surrendered heart is required for salvation. You cannot purposefully live on both sides of the fence and expect to have a heart to please God.

Chapter Nine

Choices and Accountability

When the Lord returns, He will hold us accountable for the choices we have made. In order to make the way ready for the Lord's return, the message of accountability must be preached. God never takes away man's right to make his own choices even if the choices are in direct opposition to His plan or purpose. In fact, everything in life is based on choice so it should not be a surprise salvation is also a choice. Our whole experience on earth is governed by two propositions that will determine the eternal fate of our souls. On the one hand are the things of God and all the wonderful benefits that accompany them, and on the other hand are the pleasures of sin which Satan uses to draw men away from God. Everyday we are exposed to the battle in one way or another and must make a choice which direction we will go. Salvation is not governed by automatic pilot, it is in our hands.

Deuteronomy 30:15, 19
30:15 "See, I have set before thee this day life and good, and death and evil;"
30:19 "I call Heaven and earth to record this day against you, that I have set before you life and death,

blessing and cursing: therefore choose life, that both thou and thy seed may live:"

That word still holds true today and the choice is ours whether or not we will serve the true and living God or the gods of this world. Who you choose to serve will determine where you spend eternity.

Matthew 6:24 "No man can serve two masters: for either he will hate the one, and love the other; or else he will hold to the one, and despise the other. Ye cannot serve God and mammon."

It's time for the church to take heed to the word of God. The Bible states you cannot serve two masters. Too many people are attempting to water down the word to accommodate their choices. When you love the things of the world you begin to hate the things of God. When you hold on to the things of the world you begin to despise anything standing in the way of the thing desired. For example, the last thing someone who is fornicating wants to hear is a sermon on the sin of fornication. This results in people purposefully ignoring certain parts of the Bible, making justifications to excuse their choices, living lives saturated with hypocrisy, avoiding the things of God, and abusing God's grace. They use phrases such as "I know I'm wrong, but God knows my heart," while they continue to engage in the sinful activity with no remorse or repentance. The day is approaching that they will discover that God did in fact know their heart and they will be judged by what was in it. Their love for sin was greater than their love for God.

Romans 14:12 "So then every one of us shall give account of himself to God."

We will all be held accountable for what we do on this earth. Being accountable keeps us focused on the bigger picture so that we are not distracted by the world. We are in a constant state of readiness as we await the Lord's return. He expects us to be ready and not sitting idle and caught up in the things of this world. We must never forget that we have our eyes on a better prize.

The Lord will hold his church accountable.

Matthew 13:41-42
13:41 "The Son of Man shall send forth His angels, and they shall gather out of His kingdom all things that offend, and them which do iniquity;"
13:42 "And shall cast them into a furnace of fire: there shall wailing and gnashing of teeth."

Matthew 24:44
24:44 "Therefore be ye also ready: for in such an hour as ye think not the Son of Man cometh."

Luke 21:34-36
21:34 "And take heed to yourselves, lest at any time your hearts be overcharged with surfeiting, and drunkenness, and cares of this life, and so that day come upon you unawares."
21:35 "For as a snare shall it come upon all them that dwell on the face of the whole earth."
21:36 "Watch ye therefore, and pray always, that ye may be accounted worthy to escape all these things that shall come to pass, and to stand before the Son of Man."

We have become too familiar with God as if He is merely our pal that passively stands by while we change the rules of holiness to a version that is more hip and up to date. The gospel has become a song and dance to attract members instead of winning souls.

Another Prophetic Dream
One night, as I lay in bed, the Lord showed me a very disturbing image. I saw myself standing in the middle of a schoolyard full of young people of all ages. They appeared to be uninhibited as they ran around participating in all types of ungodly behavior. I stood there and watched as they laughed and boasted. Some were smoking, drinking, and using drugs with no shame whatsoever. Others were even having sex in the open for all to see. Everything was normal to them as if they were celebrating their freedom. It didn't even matter that I was standing there. They just looked at me and laughed, absent of shame. As I continued to observe them, I realized that the young people had been turned over to a reprobate mind because they refused God's commandments. These were rebellious children that despised God and chose to live in the world.

I began to hear multiple gunshots and I saw dozens of them fall to the ground covered with blood. The others merely ran for cover stepping over the bodies of the slain. After all the shooting subsided, they merely went back to their various activities despite the many dead that lay in the yard with blood still pouring out of their bodies. There was no outrage or sadness, and the laughter continued to be heard. Their hearts were numb to feelings of human compassion and their minds had no room for remorse.

The Lord impressed upon me that these young people had to be won to Christ, as soon as possible, through compassion and love, otherwise a great deal of them would be lost.

Excerpt "Why God Kept Saving Me"

We are no longer conditioning our young people to be accountable to God or policing the floodgates of immorality; rather we have created a society overrun by images of sex and pornography, gender confusion, and violence on a daily basis. We are in danger of bringing up an entire generation of young people who do not know God and are trapped in sin because we no longer fight to preserve their innocence. The more we sit idle as our children are robbed of their innocence, the more they will turn away from God, make bad choices, doubt God, embrace alternative life styles, and adopt the behavior of the world. Hypocrisy is driving our youth into the hands of worldly icons for guidance and direction whose influences are derived from the god's of this world. At least they practice what they preach. They sing, dance, and promote sin and their lifestyles are consistent. In the minds of our youth, truth many times is measured by consistency whereas hypocrisy can even make the truth appear to be unbelievable. Failing to practice what we preach causes the truth of God to appear to be a lie. Now ask yourself Christian, is your lifestyle lying on God?

Judges 2:10 "And also all that generation were gathered unto their fathers: and there arose another generation after them, which knew not the Lord, nor yet the works which he had done for Israel."

We have become a body of watered down believers that have become high on the illusion of supernatural power, but powerless to see the true manifestations described in the Bible. For all the churches, professing Christians, prayer conferences, books, and tapes in this country, we are being outsmarted, out recruited, and out planned by the devil. We see more and more churches being built with thousands of members, but how much impact are they having on the communities in which they're located. Our schools and communities continue to grow worse. We hear about thousands of souls giving their lives to Christ, but how many are being discipled into holiness and not using the church as a revolving door?

Our country is becoming more and more immoral each day. Violence and pornography are on the rise, sacred institutions such as marriage are being attacked, our young people are exposed to tons of destructive images on a daily basis, but our attitude has been, "don't worry because there is a new church being built on the corner." What sense does this make? While Satan runs wild in the world, we continue to build more buildings to hide in.

For example, I talked with a Principal of a local middle school who expressed his disappointment in the fact that his school was located in the vicinity of several churches, and not one of them responded to his invitation to reach out to his youth.

The Bible states that we are more than conquerors and that we can do all things through Christ who strengthens us. So why do we, the church, allow Satan to continually destroy our neighborhoods and corrupt our young people while we declare His goodness behind closed doors? It is time for the body of Christ to get its hands dirty in the things of the Lord. We must be accountable to the work we were called to do. The devil has been effective at keeping our minds preoccupied with carnal things, causing many to totally miss the point when it comes to the things that are important to God. The purpose of the church is to be a fueling station, not a rest home.

Chapter Ten

The Perils of Apostasy

<u>II Chronicles 24:18-19</u>
24:18 "And they left the house of the Lord God of their fathers, and served groves and idols: and wrath came upon Judah and Jerusalem for this their trespass."
24:19 "Yet He sent prophets to them, to bring them again unto the Lord; and they testified against them: but they would not give ear."

<u>Mark 13:22</u> "For false Christs and false prophets shall rise, and shall shew signs and wonders, to seduce, if it were possible, even the elect."

<u>John 6:64</u>
6:64 "But there are some of you that believe not. For Jesus knew from the beginning who they were that believed not, and who should betray Him."

<u>John 6:70</u> "Jesus answered them, Have not I chosen you twelve, and one of you is a devil."

<u>John 12:43</u> "For they loved the praise of men more than the praise of God."

The church must get back to preaching the unadulterated word of God to ensure that each person is ready when Jesus returns. There will be those that start the race but will not finish. Only those willing to endure until the end will be ready for Jesus' triumphant return.

One might wonder why a man would come to God and later turn away from Him. The answer is simple. Not everyone confessing Jesus means it from the heart, and there are those that confess Jesus but fail to protect their heart and later fall away. The Lord not only instructed us how to receive salvation but also how to protect it. The danger of attempting to play on both sides of the fence is that your heart is exposed to those things that oppose God. Once your heart becomes infected with sin you become ripe for deception. Through compromise, reasoning, and justification you will even deceive yourself in order to hold onto the very things that God hates.

Matthew 6:24 "No man can serve two masters: for either he will hate the one, and love the other; or else he will hold to the one, and despise the other, You cannot serve God and mammon (devil)"

Consider the parable Jesus gave concerning His word in Mark 4:14-20 and how the word would be received in various ways depending on the condition of the heart:

Mark 4:14-20
4:14 "The sower soweth the word."
4:15 "And these are they by the way side, where the word is sown; but when they have heard, Satan cometh immediately, and taketh away the word that was sown in their hearts."
4:16 "And these are they likewise which are sown

on stony ground; who when they have heard the word, immediately receive it with gladness."

4:17 "And have no root in themselves, and so endure but for a time: afterward, when affliction or persecution ariseth for the word's sake, immediately they are offended."

4:18 "And these are they which are sown among thorns; such as hear the word,"

4:19 "And the cares of this world, and the deceitfulness of riches, and the lusts of other things entering in, choke the word, and it becometh unfruitful."

4:20 "And these are they which are sown on good ground; such as hear the word, and receive it, and bring forth fruit, some thirty fold, some sixty, and some an hundred."

Some words would find good soil or a right heart, and other words would find rocks and thorns or a hardened heart. The love of God produces good soil and just as the enemy seeks to steal the word from your heart, worldliness will deplete your soil. God's love produces unselfishness, accountability, charitableness, longsuffering, humility, truthfulness, hope, endurance, faith, sincere repentance, and obedience, while the love of the world results in the lust of the flesh, the lust of the eyes, and the pride of life.

Those that neglect to discover, and line up with the will of God make themselves vulnerable to the cares of this world and hardened hearts. You must protect your heart at all cost. Once your heart is hardened, the door is opened to Apostasy, or falling away from the Lord. The Lord warned us in Matthew 24:12, "And because iniquity shall abound, the love of many shall wax cold." Iniquity abounds where the will of God is not known or where people simply refuse to do His will. Today we see more and more people whose hearts have become increasingly cold towards God, and around the world iniquity abounds.

God judges by the heart of man:

I Samuel 16:7 "But the Lord said unto Samuel, Look not on his countenance, or on the height of his stature; because I have refused him: for the **Lord seeth not as man seeth**; for man looketh on the outward appearance, but the Lord looketh on the heart."

It is possible to fall away after you have received salvation if you fail to keep hold of the things of God:

I Timothy 4:1-2
4:1 "Now the Spirit speaketh expressly, that in the latter times some shall depart from the faith, giving heed to seducing spirits, and doctrines of devils;"
4:2 "Speaking lies in hypocrisy; having their conscience seared with a hot iron."

Hebrews 3:12 "Take heed, brethren, lest there be in any of you an evil heart of unbelief, in departing from the living God."

Hebrews 10:38 "Now the just shall live by faith: but if any man draw back, my soul shall have no pleasure in him."

Luke 9:62 "And Jesus said unto him, No man, having put his hand to the plough, and looking back, is fit for the kingdom of God."

John 6:66 "From that time many of His disciples went back, and walked no more with Him."

II Timothy 4:10 "For Demas hath forsaken me, having loved this present world, and is departed unto Thessalonica; Crescens to Galatia, Titus unto Dalmatia."

II Peter 3:17 "Ye therefore, beloved, seeing ye know these things before, beware lest ye also, being led away with the error of the wicked, fall from your own steadfastness."

Galatians 4:9 "But now, after that ye have known God, or rather are known of God, how turn ye again to the weak and beggarly elements, whereunto ye desire again to be in bondage?"

I John 2:18-19
2:18 "Little children, it is the last time: and as ye have heard that antichrist shall come, even now are there many antichrists; whereby we know that it is the last time."
2:19 "They went out from us, but they were not of us; for if they had been of us, they would no doubt have continued with us: but they went out, that they might be made manifest that they were not all of us."

II Peter 2:20-22
2:20 "For if after they have escaped the pollutions of the world through the knowledge of the Lord and Saviour Jesus Christ, they are again entangled therein, and overcome, the latter end is worse with them than the beginning."
2:21 "For it had been better for them not to have

known the way of righteousness, than, after they have known it, to turn from the holy commandment delivered unto them."

2:22 "But it is happened unto them according to the true proverb, The dog is turned to his own vomit again; and the sow that was washed to her wallowing in the mire."

There are certain states of sin that can cause you to lose your salvation:

a. Blasphemy of the Holy Ghost

Mark 3:29 "But he that shall blaspheme against the Holy Ghost hath never forgiveness, but is in danger of eternal damnation."

Matthew 12:31-32
12:31 "Wherefore I say unto you, All manner of sin and blasphemy shall be forgiven unto men: but the blasphemy against the Holy Ghost shall not be forgiven unto men."
12:32 "And whosoever speaketh a word against the Son of man, it shall be forgiven him: but whosoever speaketh against the Holy Ghost, it shall not be forgiven him, neither in this world, neither in the world to come."

b. Crucifying the Lord afresh

Hebrews 6:4-6
6:4 "For it is impossible for those who were once enlightened, and have tasted of the heavenly gift. And were made partakers of the Holy Ghost,"
6:5 "And have tasted the good word of God, and the powers of the world to come."
6:6 "If they shall fall away, to renew them again unto

repentance; seeing they crucify to themselves the Son of God afresh, and put Him to an open shame."

It is important to point out that falling away is not the same as committing a sin. The falling away discussed in this scripture follows an advanced state of revelation one can receive from God. This person walks away from God, His grace, His mercy, and the opportunity to repent to the point of reprobation, or he ignores the Holy Spirit to the point that he no longer has a conscience concerning sin.

c. Receiving the Mark of the Beast:

Revelation 14:9-11
14:9 " And the third angel followed them, saying with a loud voice, If any man worship the beast and his image, and receive his mark in his forehead, or in his hand."

14:10 " The same shall drink of the wine of the wrath of God, which is poured out without mixture into the cup of His indignation; and he shall be tormented with fire and brimstone in the presence of the holy angels, and in the presence of the lamb."

14:11 "And the smoke of their torment ascendeth up for ever and ever: and they have no rest day nor night, who worship the beast and his image, and whosoever receiveth the mark of his name."

Whether you subscribe to pre-tribulation or post-tribulation rapture of the church, there will still be people here on earth that must make a decision concerning Jesus. There may even be those that make a decision to accept Jesus but in the face of persecution choose to turn away.

d. Purposefully mishandling the Word of God:

Revelation 22:18-19
22:18 "For I testify unto every man that heareth the words of the prophecy of this book, If any man shall add unto these things, God shall add unto him the plagues that are written in this book:

22:19 "And if any man shall take away from the words of the book of this prophecy, God shall take away his part out of the book of life, and out of the holy city, and from the things which are written in this book."

The perils of Apostasy:

The more we water down the word, refuse to be accountable for our actions, cling to a personal relationship with God that is not Biblically based, and make justifications to live worldly lives, the more we play right into the enemy's hand. We live in a day characterized by the very falling away spoken of in the Bible. This falling away will ultimately pave the way for the anti-christ through the creation of a society that is anti-God. We have become a society that loves pleasure more than we love God. We have become drunk in our own deceit; claiming to be wise we have become as fools.

It is one thing for the world to behave this way, but quite another when those that profess Jesus Christ fall victim to the same deceitful thinking. A divided house cannot stand and when people begin writing their own Bible under the guise of interpretation and intellectualism the end result is division, chaos, and confusion. Despite the various versions and dialects the Bible is written in, the meaning is not lost in the translation or interpretation. It is not a secret code that only a privileged few can understand, and you cannot bend, twist, and manipulate the word to accommodate your choices; rather the word is supposed to govern your choices. It is a dangerous proposition to suggest that any parts of the Bible are incorrect. This sort of thinking has already resulted in countless denominations, suggestions that words don't mean what they say, and people that choose to view the Bible as a mere reference point in order to avoid being confused and manipulated. I say again that the Bible is the undisputed word of God that is either 100% correct or 100% wrong.

Matthew 12:25 "And Jesus knew their thoughts, and said unto them, Every kingdom divided against itself is brought to desolation; and every city or house divided against itself shall not stand."

I Corinthians 1:10 "Now I beseech you, brethren, by the name of our Lord Jesus Christ, that ye all speak the same thing, and that there be no divisions among you; but that ye be perfectly joined together in the same mind and in the same judgment."

Keep it simple. The gospel was made to enlighten people not to confuse them:

I Corinthians 1:17-20
1:17 "For Christ sent me not to baptize, but to preach the gospel: not with wisdom of words, lest the cross of Christ should be made of none effect."
1:18 "For the preaching of the cross is to them that perish foolishness; but unto us which are saved it is the power of God."
1:19 "For it is written, I will destroy the wisdom of the

wise, and will bring to nothing the understanding of the prudent."

1:20 "Where is the wise? Where is the scribe? Where is the disputer of this world? Hath not God made foolish the wisdom of this world?"

This is not an indictment against wisdom; rather it is an indictment against man relying on his own wisdom and not the wisdom of God. The reason why God sent the Holy Ghost was because He knew that we needed a teacher and a guide. The more we stray from the leading of the Holy Ghost the more susceptible we become to apostasy.

Relying on man's wisdom leads to apostasy.
One of the ways Satan has been effective at infiltrating the church is by selling the church on the illusion that we are smarter than the children of the world. In the pursuit of good ideas, self gratification, and zeal to save the world more and more Christians are straying away from the yea and nay of the word and the guidance of the Holy Ghost, choosing rather to rely on their own insight and understanding. In other words, too many people in the church believe they can play with fire and not get burnt.

Luke 16:8 "And the Lord commended the unjust steward, because he had done wisely: for the children of this world are in their generation wiser than the children of light."

We dibble and dabble in the world, embrace their music, imitate their lifestyles, adopt their ways of thinking, impersonate their celebrities, and assume that just because we're carrying a Bible we're out of harm's way. Satan has discovered that many saints think fruit is simply something that grows on a tree which has allowed him to transform his demons into angels of light undetected. He continues to prove that he knows a lot more about taking advantage of us than we know about defeating him.

The smarter we get the blinder we become. More and more professing saints are abandoning sound doctrine choosing rather to adopt worldly principles and values that afford them greater freedom to make their own choices, even if those choices are not lined up with the word of God. The result is a slippery slope where we now witness professing Christians boldly challenging the divinity of Christ and the virgin birth, defending same sex marriages and alternative lifestyles under the banner of love. Abortions are justified in the interest of choice and lifestyles are lived contrary to the teachings of Jesus. All of this is done while promoting the belief that the Bible is simply a reference point that does not have to be followed to the letter. Even the notion of love is increasingly distorted to embrace the belief that there are no consequences for our actions, nor any judgment for sin.

God has no love for unrighteousness:

II Thessalonians 2:11-12
2:11 "And for this cause God shall send them strong delusion, that they should believe a lie."
2:12 "That they all might be damned who believed not the truth, but had pleasure in unrighteousness."

Christians that choose to boldly stand on the word of God are increasingly seen as intolerant, insensitive, and hate mongers promoting an exclusionary ideology. The situation is made worse by the contradiction posed by professing Christians whose lifestyles and beliefs mirror the world. Instead of convicting the world they afford them greater credibility. This leaves others with the impression that Christianity is a schizophrenic religion full of hypocrisy and hate. There are those that give people the idea that once they profess Jesus they can live any way they choose and still remain in fellowship with God which is a first class ticket to the world of apostasy. The minute you take away accountability from salvation you open the floodgates for falling away. Some people without realizing it become apostates by the very nature of their lifestyles.

Reliance on the World leads to apostasy.

<u>II. Chronicles 16:2-3, 7-9</u>
16:2 "Then Asa brought out silver and gold out of the treasures of the house of the Lord and out of the king's house, and sent to Benhadad king of Syria, that dwelt at Damascus, saying,"

16:3 "There is a league between me and thee, as there was between my father and thy father: behold I have sent thee silver and gold; go break thy league with Baasha king of Israel, that he may depart from me."

16:7 "And at that time Hanani the seer came to Asa king of Judah, and said unto him, Because thou hast relied on the king of Syria, and not relied on the Lord thy God, therefore is the host of the king of Syria escaped out of thine hand."

16:8 "Were not the Lubims a huge host, with very many chariots and horsemen? Yet, because thou didst rely on the Lord, He delivered them into thine hand."

16:9 "For the eyes of the Lord run to and fro throughout the whole earth, to shew Himself strong in the behalf of them whose heart is perfect toward Him. Herein thou hast done foolishly: therefore from henceforth thou shalt have wars."

More and more churches are falling into the trap of trying to be like the world in order to win the world to Jesus. The walls that once divided the sanctification of the church from the spirit of worldliness are being replaced by a disturbing alliance between the church and the world. Not only does this rob God of His glory, it enables the world to gain access to His most precious treasure, our souls. The world is not supposed to receive any credit for winning souls to Jesus which is exactly what happens when we compromise standards of holiness in order to attract people into the church, especially when it comes to youth. Although you may be successful in getting Jesus in their mouth you have done nothing to get the world out of their heart. It would be better to have one person receive Jesus in his heart than for ten people to confess Jesus while caught up in the moment or simply having a good time.

Apostasy is falling away from Jesus which means that a relationship once existed which was later severed. The only way the enemy can cause a person to fall away from Jesus is that he must first gain access and then enter into the relationship himself. When we mix sanctification with worldliness we give Satan an open door into the very marriage we have with Jesus. Apostasy is spiritual adultery.

James 4:4 "Ye adulterers and adulteresses, know ye not that the friendship of the world is enmity with God? Whosoever therefore will be a friend of the world is the enemy of God."

Sanctification and holiness have a distinct purpose

in the church. They are God's covering over the very relationship we have with Jesus. The devil knows the Bible and can appear to be an angel of light, but he cannot live holy. Sanctification, or setting ourselves apart from the world, is not a denomination; rather it is the first line of defense against the forces of Satan. It is the only way to spot the intruder and flush him out.

Deception leads to apostasy.
The Bible warns us of the deception that is to mark the last days. Matthew 24:24 states, "For there shall arise false Christs, and false prophets, and shall shew great signs and wonders; insomuch that, if it were possible, they shall deceive the very elect." Now ask yourself, "Are you more likely to be deceived if you strictly adhere to the word of God, or if you rely on your own insight to pick and choose which parts of the Bible to receive or reject?' I propose eternity is too great a risk to take by clinging to a roll of the dice mentality when it comes to serving God.

For those readers that find these statements extreme, consider the warnings given in the Bible concerning the days we are living in.

II Thessalonians 2:3 "Let no man deceive you by any means: for that day shall not come, except there come a falling away first, and that man of sin be revealed, the son of perdition;"

II Timothy 2:2-5
2:2 "Preach the word; be instant in season, out of season; reprove, rebuke, exhort with all longsuffering and doctrine."
2:3 "For the time will come when they will not endure sound doctrine; but after their own lusts shall they heap to themselves teachers, having itching ears;"

2:4 "And they shall turn away their ears from the truth, and shall be turned unto fables."

2:5 "But watch thou in all things, endure afflictions, do the work of an evangelist, make full proof of thy ministry."

<u>II Timothy 3:1-7</u>
3:1 "This know also, that in the last days perilous times shall come."

3:2 "For men shall be lovers of their own selves, covetous, boasters, proud, blasphemers, disobedient to parents, unthankful, unholy."

3:3 "Without natural affection, trucebreakers, false accusers, incontinent, fierce, despisers of those that are good."

3:4 "Traitors, heady, high minded, lovers of pleasures more than lovers of God;"

3:5 "Having a form of godliness, but denying the power thereof: from such turn away."

3:6 "For of this sort are they which creep into houses, and lead captive silly women laden with sins, led away with divers lusts,"

3:7 "Ever learning, and never able to come to the knowledge of the truth."

<u>II Timothy 3:12-14</u>
3:12 "Yea, and all that will live godly in Christ Jesus shall suffer persecution."

3:13 "But evil men and seducers shall wax worse, deceiving, and being deceived."

3:14 "But continue thou in the things which thou hast learned and hast been assured of, knowing of whom thou hast learned them;"

I Peter 2:1-3

2:1 "But there were false prophets also among the people, even as there shall be false teachers among you, who privily shall bring in damnable heresies, even denying the Lord that bought them, and bring upon themselves swift destruction."

2:2 "And many shall follow their pernicious ways; by reason of whom the way of truth shall be evil spoken of;"

2:3 "And through covetousness shall they with feigned words make merchandise of you: whose judgment now of a long time lingereth not, and their damnation slumbereth not."

The Holy Ghost

When I woke up Monday morning, I was looking for the love of God. As usual, my first stop was the prayer closet. I sat down like I always did and closed the door. As I began to talk with God, I found myself entering into a deep conversation with Him. I began to feel like I was floating and I no longer felt the floor beneath me. There were no walls where I was sitting and the space around me appeared to be limitless. I began to talk faster and faster and words began to fill my mouth as if I was listening to someone else. I had no idea where the words were coming from as they rolled off of my lips one after the other. I cannot even recall everything I said. I only remember the conversation being very focused and intense. A force began to erupt from my belly. It felt like rain and wind were falling upon me even though the rain was not wet but rather drops of air. My eyes were closed but I sensed that it came from the ceiling and descended on me with miraculous force. When it came in, I was immediately pushed out. It felt as if I was pushed to the most remote areas of my mind to observe what was going on. I knew that I had been inhabited because I no longer had any control over my body and I was merely there as an observer. My hands flew up in the air and it felt like electricity was rushing through my body. Even though I had never been electrocuted, the characteristics of electricity were the first thing that came to my mind. My body was completely overpowered and supercharged with energy from my head to my feet. Every muscle in my body felt stimulated and my body began to shake as if I was suspended in air. The wind rushed into my body, and then came rushing back out. I began to speak in a foreign language with such force and intensity it scared me. My body was being shaken, and the language was forced out of my belly. I began to wonder how much my body could physically take. I felt completely powerless as I sat back and witnessed this phenomenal event. Something kept telling me to just relax and witness the power of God. The Holy Ghost then said "I AM HERE," and scriptures came to my remembrance that told me the sounds I heard were the Holy Ghost uttering ancient tongues. As He moved through me, I was amazed at my complete lack of control and my fears began to rise up against me. I was frightened at first because I felt a presence in the room with me and it was not only around me, but in me as well. Even though I knew this was the Holy Ghost, it was still the most amazing thing I had ever witnessed in my life. After about half an hour of speaking in tongues and being electrocuted in the spirit, I felt like I gracefully reentered my body. I do not think I literally left my body, but I was temporarily out of control, which was something I had never before experienced.

When it was all over, I had tremendous joy coupled with utter amazement. I sat in the closet looking around in disbelief. I could not believe what had just happened to me and I sat there thinking "Wow!" Nothing that happened hurt me in any way. In fact, it was the opposite. It was the best thing I had ever felt. I just was not used to not having any control over my body and being engulfed by the presence of God. I felt God all around me as if He was holding me in His hands. This was beyond words in explanation. I had experienced the awesome power of the Holy Ghost while sitting in a remote place in my mind. My body had been physically overwhelmed and I felt the activity of electricity totally subjecting anything in its path as it traveled through my body.

I slowly stood up and walked out of the closet filled with joy. It took me a few minutes to come down from the high I experienced and get acclimated to my room. Everything was quiet and motionless, which was the exact opposite of what I had experienced.

Excerpt: "Why God Kept Saving Me"

Chapter Eleven

The Power Source

Once you are saved, the single most important thing in your Christian walk is to be filled with the Holy Ghost, evidenced by speaking in tongues. The Holy Ghost will manifest power in your life to live saved and be an effective witness in the world. He also enables you to speak in a heavenly language that results in intercession on your behalf and the behalf of others. The Holy Ghost will give you boldness you have never before experienced, and you will see the world in an entirely different light. The power of the Holy Ghost will propel you out of the rocking chair of complacency and into the battle.

The purpose of this chapter is to present Biblical support concerning the role of the Holy Ghost and proof that speaking in tongues was not confined to the Disciples in the book of Acts. The power of the Holy Ghost is a free gift from God available to all that have accepted Jesus Christ as their Lord and Savior. To be victorious in the last days, it will be critical to be filled with the Holy Ghost. This is the power that has been given to the church to prepare the way of our Lord.

The devil has used a lack of understanding, fear, and man made doctrine to deny believers the one thing that will utterly destroy his works in the earth which is an on-fire church filled with the Holy Ghost and power. We use this power to live saved, deny the flesh, have victory over the workings of the devil, conquer fear, pray God's will into the earth, and snatch those that are lost out of the devil's grasp.

It should be evident by now we don't need more churches in our communities, but more Holy Ghost filled believers. In some areas, we have churches on every corner but the neighborhoods surrounding them are war zones over run with drugs, violence, and poverty. This is not what God intended; when we profess we have got the devil under our feet. Many churches have simply become places of escape from the world as opposed to command centers instructing people how to change the world.

God never intended for the world to chase us into hiding; rather we are supposed to have authority over the territory the Lord has placed us in. A Holy Ghost filled church will possess the authority to take back the lands the devil has captured and drive him out. Deuteronomy 32:30 states that with the Lord on our side, one can chase a thousand and two can put ten thousand to flight so retreat is not an option. Additionally, the power of the Holy Ghost can't be confined to simply falling out in the pews on Sunday morning and dancing because we're happy. We need to take the power of the Holy Ghost into the streets the same way the disciples did in the book of Acts. A Holy Ghost filled believer becomes a one-man army in his home, on his job, at the grocery store, and anywhere else he travels while eagerly waiting for opportunities for the Lord to show Himself strong.

Every believer must know what the word says concerning the Holy Ghost and accept this precious gift God made available. The discussion should not be based on opinion or denominational doctrines but simply faith and a belief in what the Word says. A lack of faith is the main reason people fall short when it comes to the manifestation of God's power in their lives. You must take God at His Word and have the faith to believe what He says.

The account of how I experienced the baptism of the Holy Ghost is true right down to the periods closing each thought. I spent years in the world running from God never knowing of this miraculous power to keep me. Because I was never taught against the Holy Ghost, it made it easier for me to believe. I did not even understand His purpose but I was eager and excited to learn. All I knew was from the moment I surrendered my life to Jesus Christ, I wanted everything promised to me by God. When they showed me in the word that I could be filled with the Holy Ghost, the matter was settled and I was determined to receive. The only thing I took into the closet with me the day I received the Holy Ghost was faith in what the word said. It was on the strength of that faith that the Lord filled me, and He will do the same for you!

It is also important to point out that everyone may not have the same experience as I described. I have seen people filled with the Holy Ghost in a variety of different ways and expressions. Some are demonstrative and some are not. Some feel a lot and others feel very little. Some tarry for the Holy Ghost and others are filled instantly. The bottom line is it doesn't matter how you get filled. Simply surrender your life to God, ask Him for the gift, and exercise your faith to receive. You don't have to beg because the gift is yours and God wants you to have it. You will be able to begin enjoying the benefits immediately regardless as to what you may feel, see, or, hear at the time.

I am a firm believer that if it's in the Bible, then it

needs to be preached. Philippians 2:12 states, "Wherefore, my beloved, as ye have always obeyed, not as in my presence only, but now much more in my absence, work out your own salvation with fear and trembling." Believers must take personal responsibility for getting into the Word for themselves and acting on it. If there are those that still don't believe, then allow the Holy Ghost to bear witness of Himself through you.

Romans 3:3-4

3:3 "For what if some did not believe? Shall their unbelief make the faith of God without effect?"

3:4 "God forbid: yea, let God be true, but every man a liar; as it is written, That thou mightest be justified in thy sayings, and mightest overcome when thou art judged."

The Holy Ghost, also called the Spirit of Truth, the Holy Spirit, and the Comforter, is the third member of the trinity and has many functions such as: intercession on our behalf and the behalf of others, praying out the will and mysteries of God into the earth, comforting the body of Christ, reproving the world of sin, righteousness, and judgment, bringing things to our remembrance, guiding and directing us into all truth, bearing witness of the Lord Jesus Christ, teaching us, giving us revelation and understanding, and manifesting the power of God in our lives including: boldness, miracles, signs and wonders, manifestation of the fruits of the Spirit, healings, and other demonstrations of the power of God.

Most people believe in the Holy Ghost as the third member of the trinity, but some fail to believe the Holy Ghost is manifesting the same power today through men and women of God that He did in the lives of the disciples in the book of Acts.

Let us consider what the word says concerning the role of the Holy Ghost, the importance of tongues, whether or not the experience was limited to the disciples, and how it is God's will you be filled with the Holy Ghost today.

God anointed Jesus Christ with the Holy Ghost and with power and Jesus Christ declared that our works as believers would exceed His:

Acts 10:38 "How God anointed Jesus of Nazareth with the Holy Ghost and with power: who went about doing good, and healing all that were oppressed of the devil; for God was with Him."

Luke 4:1 "And Jesus being full of the Holy Ghost returned from Jordan, and was led by the Spirit into the wilderness."

John 14:12 "Verily, verily, I say unto you, He that believeth on me, the works that I do shall he do also: and greater works than these shall he do; because I go unto my Father."

Acts 1:1-2
1:1 "The former treatise have I made, O Theophilus, of all that Jesus began both to do and teach."
1:2 "Until the day in which He was taken up, after that He through the Holy Ghost had given commandments unto the apostles He had chosen"

In Luke 4:1 Jesus left instruction that believers would do greater works than He did. If the Bible tells us Jesus was anointed by the Holy Ghost and with power to perform these great works, wouldn't it also follow that if we are supposed to do even greater works, we would have to be anointed with the same power? This instruction was not given for the Disciples alone: it was given to those that "believeth" on Jesus Christ.

Jesus said greater works than these shall we do

because He went to be with the Father. When Jesus gave this instruction, the work of the cross had not yet been accomplished. It was important for Him to finish the work of the cross so He could dwell on the inside of us. Man was still dead in sin, thus the Holy Ghost could not dwell on the inside. In those days He was manifested by coming on people and empowering them for a particular task, but did not dwell on the inside of men.

The promise:

John 16:7-11
16:7 "Nevertheless I tell you the truth; It is expedient for you that I go away: for if I go not away, the Comforter will not come unto you; but if I depart, I will send Him unto you."
16:8 "And when He is come, He will reprove the world of sin, and of righteousness, and of judgment:"
16:9 "Of sin, because they believe not on me;"
16:10 "Of righteousness, because I go to my Father, and ye see me no more;"
16:11 "Of judgment, because the prince of this world is judged."

John 15:26 " But when the comforter is come, whom I will send unto you from the Father, even the Spirit of Truth, which proceedeth from the Father, He shall testify of me."

John 14:16-17
14:16 "And I will pray the Father, and He shall give you another Comforter, that he may abide with you for ever."
14:17 "Even the Spirit of truth; whom the world cannot

receive, because it seeth him not, neither knoweth him; for he dwelleth with you, and shall be in you".

I John 2:27 "But the anointing which ye have received of Him abideth in you, and ye need not that any man teach you: but as the same anointing teacheth you of all things, and is truth, and is no lie, and even as it hath taught you, ye shall abide in Him."

John 16:13-14
16:13 "Howbeit when he, the Spirit of Truth, is come, he will guide you into all truth: for he shall not speak of himself; but whatsoever he shall hear, that shall he speak: and will shew you things to come."
16:14 "He shall glorify me: for he shall receive of mine, and shall shew it unto you."

John 14:26 "But the comforter, which is the Holy Ghost, whom the father will send in my name, He shall teach you all things, and bring all things to your remembrance, whatsoever I have said unto you."

Luke 12:12 "For the Holy Ghost will teach you in that same hour what ye ought to say"

The promise was made even before Jesus Christ was manifested in the flesh:

A. John the Baptist foretold the baptism of the Holy Ghost.

Matthew 3:11 "I indeed baptize you with water unto repentance: but He that cometh after me is mightier than

I, whose shoes I am not worthy to bear: He shall baptize you with the Holy Ghost, and with fire."

B. The Prophet Joel prophesied the baptism of the Holy Ghost in the Old Testament.

Joel 2:28 "And it shall come to pass afterward, that I will pour out my spirit upon all flesh; and your sons and your daughters shall prophesy, your old men shall dream dreams, your young men shall see visions."

The gift is available to those that have received Jesus Christ and have the faith to ask God for the gift of the Holy Ghost.

Luke 11:13 "If ye then, being evil, know how to give good gifts unto your children: how much more shall your heavenly Father give the Holy Spirit to them that ask Him?"

Once Jesus finished the work of the cross, and man had been redeemed from sin through His blood, the Holy Ghost now had access to live on the inside. The Lord Jesus Christ promised the Holy Ghost or Comforter to all believers.

The Lord Jesus Christ renewed the promise after the work of the cross had been completed.

Acts 1:4-5

1:4 "And, being assembled together with them, commanded them that they should not depart from Jerusalem, but wait for the promise of the Father, which, saith He, ye have heard of Me."

1:5 "For John truly baptized with water; but ye shall be baptized with the Holy Ghost not many days hence."

Acts 1:8 "But ye shall receive power, after that the Holy Ghost is come upon you: and ye shall be witnesses unto me both in Jerusalem, and in all Judea, and in Samaria, and unto the uttermost part of the earth."

The promise was fulfilled on the Day of Pentecost and one hundred and twenty Disciples of Christ were filled with the gift of the Holy Ghost. This was the first instance of the filling of the Holy Ghost but most definitely was not the last.

Acts 2: 1-4
2:1 "And when the day of Pentecost was fully come, they were all with one accord in one place."
2:2 "And suddenly there came a sound from heaven as of a rushing mighty wind, and it filled all the house where they were sitting."
2:3 "And there appeared unto them cloven tongues like as of fire, and it sat upon each of them."
2:4 "And they were all filled with the Holy Ghost, and began to speak with other tongues, as the Spirit gave them utterance."

Acts 4:8 "Then Peter, filled with the Holy Ghost, said unto them, Ye rulers of the people, and elders of Israel."

Acts 13:9 "Then Saul (who is also called Paul,) filled with the Holy Ghost, set his eyes on him."

Acts 13:52 "And the disciples were filled with joy, and with the Holy Ghost."

Once the Disciples were filled, they boldly preached to others about the Lord Jesus Christ and the wonderful gift of the Holy Ghost. The experience was not just limited to the original disciples filled on the Day of Pentecost, but to all that believed on the Lord Jesus Christ, Jews and Gentiles alike. The Gentiles were non-Jews that were not Disciples of Christ, yet because of their belief in Jesus Christ they were also filled with the Holy Ghost. Notice the word whosoever in Acts 10:43. The Bible says "whosoever believeth on Him" could receive the gift and those that believed were filled with the Holy Ghost. Once they received remission of sins through the blood of Jesus, they were eligible to receive the gift of the Holy Ghost. If that is the case, why would anyone allow someone to stand in the way of them being filled with the Holy Ghost if they are included in "whosoever?" Once again the Bible is the final authority on the matter and not the opinions of men.

Acts 10:43-48

10:43 "To Him give all the prophets witness, that through His name **whosoever** believeth in Him shall receive remission of sins."

10:44 "While Peter yet spake these words, the Holy Ghost fell on all them which heard the word."

10:45 "And they of the circumcision which believed were astonished, as many as came with Peter, because that on the Gentiles, also was poured out the gift of the Holy Ghost."

10:46 "For they heard them speak with tongues, and magnify God. Then answered Peter."

10:47 "Can any man forbid water, that these should not be baptized, which have received the Holy Ghost as well as we?"

10:48 "And he commanded them to be baptized in the

name of the Lord. Then prayed they him to tarry certain days."

Many others received the gift of the Holy Ghost:

Acts 2:38 "And Peter said unto them, Repent, and be baptized every one of you in the name of Jesus Christ for the remission of sins, and ye shall receive the gift of the Holy Ghost."

Acts 4:31 "And when they had prayed, the place was shaken where they were assembled together; and they were all filled with the Holy Ghost, and they spake the word of God with boldness."

Acts 5:32 "And we are His witnesses of these things; and so is also the Holy Ghost, whom God hath given to them that obey Him."

Acts 8:17 "Then laid they their hands on them, and they received the Holy Ghost."

Acts 19:6 "And when Paul had laid his hands upon them, the Holy Ghost came on them; and they spake with tongues, and prophesied."

Acts 11:24 "For he was a good man, and full of the Holy Ghost and of faith: and much people was added unto the Lord."

Acts 7:55 "But he, being full of the Holy Ghost, looked up steadfastly into heaven, and saw the glory of God, and Jesus standing on the right hand of God."

Intercession of the Holy Ghost according to the will of God:

Romans 8:26-27

8:26 "Likewise the Spirit also helpeth our infirmities: for we know not what we should pray for as we ought: but the Spirit Himself maketh intercession for us with groanings which cannot be uttered."

8:27 "And he that searcheth the hearts knoweth what is the mind of the Spirit, because He maketh intercession for the saints according to the will of God."

Chapter Twelve

The Importance of Tongues

Tongues are a manifestation of the Holy Ghost and the evidence of His indwelling. They are also one of the signs that follow them that believe in the Lord Jesus Christ.

Mark 16:17 "And these signs shall follow them that believe; In my name shall they cast out devils; they shall speak with new tongues"

Acts 2:1-4
2:1 "And when the day of Pentecost was fully come, they were all with one accord in one place."
2:2 "And suddenly there came a sound from heaven as of a rushing mighty wind, and it filled all the house where they were sitting."
2:3 "And there appeared unto them cloven tongues like as of fire, and it sat upon each of them."
2:4 "And they were all filled with the Holy Ghost, and began to speak with other tongues, as the Spirit gave them utterance."

Tongues are spoken in a variety of different languages

and can and should be exercised by every Holy Ghost filled believer.

Acts 2:6-8

2:6 "Now when this was noised abroad, the multitude came together, and were confounded because that every man heard them speak in his own language."

2:7 "And they were all amazed and marveled, saying one to another, Behold, are not all these which speak Galileans?"

2:8 "And how hear we every man in our own tongue, wherein we were born?"

Note the emphasis of the word "heard." One purpose of tongues is being a sign to unbelievers but how can unbelievers hear them if they are never spoken?

Acts 2:32-33

2:32 "This Jesus hath God raised up, whereof we are all witnesses."

2:33 " Therefore being by the right hand of God exalted, and having received of the Father the promise of the Holy Ghost, He hath shed forth this, which ye now see and hear."

I. Corinthians 14:22
Wherefore tongues are for a sign, not to them that believe, but to them that believe not: but prophesying [serveth] not for them that believe not, but for them which believe.

Not only was this the fulfillment of scripture but it was a witness to all those that did not believe. Over and over people that were filled with the Holy Ghost spoke with tongues. It was not limited to the disciples only.

Acts 19:6-7
19:6 "And when the Apostle Paul had laid his hands upon them, the Holy Ghost came on them; and they spake with tongues, and prophesied."
19:7 "And all the men were about twelve."

In I. Corinthians 12:4-10, the Apostle Paul taught on the gifts of the Spirit and the various manifestations. Every gift is for a purpose that is spelled out in the Bible. Diverse kinds of tongues are one of these gifts.

I Corinthians 12:4-10
12:4 "Now there are diversities of gifts but the same Spirit."
12:5 "And there are differences of administrations, but the same Lord."
12:6 "And there are diversities of operations, but it is the same God which worketh all in all."
12:7 "But the manifestation of the Spirit is given to every man to profit withal."
12:8 "For to one is given by the Spirit the word of wisdom; to another the word of knowledge by the same Spirit."
12:9 "To another faith by the same Spirit; to another the gifts of healing by the same Spirit."
12:10 "To another the working of miracles; to another prophecy; to another discerning of spirits; to another divers kinds of tongues; to another the interpretation of tongues."

Note—verse 12:7 above "given to every man to profit" How can you profit from something that you never use?
Each gift is important and necessary for the body of

Christ to function. We must discern our particular gift(s) and then use them to build God's kingdom.

<u>I Corinthians 12:14-22</u>

12:14 "For the body is not one member, but many."

12:15 "If the foot shall say, Because I am not the hand, I am not of the body; is it therefore not of the body."

12:16 "And if the ear shall say, Because I am not the eye, I am not of the body; is it therefore not of the body?"

12:17 "If the whole body were an eye, where were the hearing? If the whole were hearing, where were the smelling."

12:18 "But now hath God set the members every one of them in the body, as it hath pleased Him."

12:19 "And if they were all one member, where were the body?"

12:20 "But now are they many members, yet but one body."

12:21 "And the eye cannot say unto the hand, I have no need of thee: nor again the head to the feet, I have no need of you."

12:22 "Nay, much more those members of the body, which seem to be more feeble, are necessary."

<u>I Corinthians 12:28</u> "And God hath set some in the church, first apostles, secondarily prophets, thirdly teachers, after that miracles, then gifts of healings, helps, governments, diversities of tongues."

Order in the church:

<u>I Corinthians 14:13-19</u>

14:13 "Wherefore let him that speaketh in an unknown tongue pray that he may interpret."

14:14 "For if I pray in an unknown tongue, my spirit prayeth, but my understanding is unfruitful."

14:15 "What is it then? I will pray with the Spirit, and I will pray with the understanding also: I will sing with the Spirit, and I will sing with the understanding also."

14:16 " Else when thou shalt bless with the Spirit, how shall he that occupieth the room of the unlearned say Amen at thy giving of thanks, seeing he understandeth not what thou sayest?"

14:17 "For thou verily givest thanks well, but the other is not edified."

14:18 "I thank my God, I speak with tongues more than ye all:"

14:19 "Yet in church I had rather speak five words with my understanding, that by my voice I might teach others also, than ten thousand words in an unknown tongue."

<u>I Corinthians 14:27-28</u>

14:27 "If any man speak in an unknown tongue, let it be by two, or at the most by three, and that by course; and let one interpret."

14:28 "But if there be no interpreter, let him keep silence in the church; and let him speak to himself, and to God."

God is not the author of confusion so along with the gifts is the responsibility to use them wisely.

The primary purpose of tongues is self-edification whereas the primary purpose of the gift of prophecy is to edify others. That is why it is better to prophesy in a group setting such as a church because the Word spoken can edify other believers. In your personal prayer life, you should actively pray in tongues because this is a time for self-edification and intercession. When you pray in tongues, you are not only edifying yourself, but you are also praying God's will into the earth, and allowing the Holy Ghost to intercede through you on the behalf of others.

In I Corinthians 14:18-19 the Apostle Paul states that in his personal prayer life he speaks in tongues more than anyone, but in the church it is more important to edify others; thus if there is no interpreter, you are better off speaking in your primary language. The key is to consider whether or not you are communicating to God or edifying others. Tongues are appropriate in a group setting when an interpreter is present. Paul is not forbidding the church to speak in tongues, but is instructing them how to exercise spiritual gifts in a way that is decent and in order. For example, if I say, "don't everyone talk at one time," I am not forbidding people to talk. I am merely trying to create an orderly environment. There is a definite time and place for tongues as a sign for unbelievers. We are even encouraged to pray for the gift of interpretation.

<u>I Corinthians 14:22</u> "Wherefore tongues are for a sign, not to them that believe, but to them that believe not: but prophesying serveth not for them that believe not, but for them which believe."

There are also instructions concerning the descent and orderly way to exercise the gift of prophecy in the church. Are we then going to say that he is instructing the church not to prophesy? Of course not, the same way that he is not instructing believers against speaking in tongues.

The main points can be summed up in the following two verses:

I Corinthians 14:33
14:33 "For God is not the author of confusion, but of peace, as in all churches of the saints."

I Corinthians 14:40 "Let all things be done decently and in order."

The Bible tells us that tongues are unctioned by the Holy Ghost when you pray in the Spirit, and one of the primary functions of the gift of tongues is intercession on your behalf and on the behalf of others.

Acts 2:4 "And they were all filled with the Holy Ghost, and began to speak with other tongues, as the Spirit gave them utterance."

The Holy Ghost prays through you with utterances (tongues) that you would not normally utter; "tongues are a Heavenly language." The Holy Ghost not only "helpeth our infirmities" but will also pray for those things that you may not be aware of to pray for yourself. Once again tongues are spoken through the Holy Ghost.

Romans 8:26-27
8:26 "Likewise the Spirit also helpeth our infirmities: for we know not what we should pray for as we ought: but the Spirit Himself maketh intercession for us with groanings which cannot be uttered."
8:27 "And he that searcheth the hearts knoweth what is the mind of the Spirit, because He maketh intercession for the saints according to the will of God"

Bound by Lust

Satan not only was meeting me at the bar, but every foul spirit I had exposed my mind to while I was in the streets followed me home and walked right through the front door with me. In order to stop some of the arguments, I began to curtail my time at happy hour. I found myself driven to the Internet as an outlet. I would stay up all night sitting in my living room looking at tons and tons of pornographic material.

Lust is a spirit, therefore it didn't matter if I had just had sex because the lusty thoughts and impulses still bombarded my thinking. I fought and fought against the feelings and thoughts each time I turned on the computer, but felt powerless to cut it off. My flesh and inner man continued to struggle against each other. The risk of being exposed as a fake was becoming more and more a certainty.

Excerpt: "Why God Kept Saving Me"

Chapter Thirteen

Breaking the Spirit of Lust

The Spirit of lust is one of the chief hindrances that Satan uses against the body of Christ. Lust, so prevalent in the world, is the driving force behind worldly association and activities and serves as a significant deterrent from doing God's work. Achieving victory over the spirit of lust is critical if we, as a church, are going to pave the way for Jesus.

We live in a society that has become saturated in promiscuity and each day bombards us with numerous images that have lust at its roots. Lust is not just sexual but it is also a love and desire for the things of the world as opposed to the things of God. The Bible gives us repeated warnings to refrain from the lusts of the flesh. It further teaches us not to place ourselves in situations that give rise to the spirit of lust, in activities that nurture this spirit, in conversations that are lust driven, and how to guard our hearts and minds from lust and its influences.

To the extent that we, as Christians, function in this world, it is not possible to completely avoid the spirit of lust, but by making the right decisions we can significantly diminish our exposure. By adhering to the instructions God has given us concerning separation from the world and having the mind of Jesus, this can be accomplished.

Through Jesus, we have been given victory over lust if we walk in the Spirit as opposed to the flesh.

Romans 13:14 "But put ye on the Lord Jesus Christ, and make no provision for the flesh, to fulfill the lusts thereof"

I Peter 2:11 "Dearly beloved, I beseech you as strangers and pilgrims, abstain from fleshy lusts, which war against the soul"

Titus 2:12 "Teaching us that, denying ungodliness and worldly lusts, we should live soberly, righteously, and godly in this present world"

Romans 8:4-8
8:4 "That the righteousness of the law might be fulfilled in us, who walk not after the flesh, but after the Spirit"
8:5 "For they that are after the flesh do mind the things of the flesh; but they that are after the Spirit the things of the Spirit."
8:6 "For to be carnally minded is death; but to be spiritually minded is life and peace"
8:7 "Because the carnal mind is enmity against God: for it is not subject to the law of God, neither indeed can be"
8:8 "So then they that are in the flesh cannot please God."

Galatians 5:16 "This I say then, Walk in the Spirit, and ye shall not fulfill the lusts of the flesh"

<u>I Peter 4:2</u> "That he no longer should live the rest of his time in the flesh to the lusts of men, but to the will of God"

When dealing with the spirit of lust, a person must be willing to do whatever it takes to drive it out. Many people have a hard time identifying this spirit because in the world it is camouflaged and deceivingly packaged as love and attraction. Men are conditioned to pursue sexual conquest, and more and more women find nothing wrong with exploiting their bodies for profit or as a means to get attention. Even professing Christians find nothing wrong with wearing less and showing more. We have become a society of boastful people taunting our exploits in the face of God under the banner of liberty and sexual freedom. The voice of spiritual reasoning grows dull as it is drowned out by chants of "old fashioned" and "religious fanatic," but ask yourself, is society getting better or worse the more we dance to the beat of the world? What are the impact looser morals and values have had on our younger generation, our family structure and sacred institutions, such as marriage? It's amazing how we work so hard teaching our children the importance of being leaders and not followers, and how to avoid negative peer pressure. At the same time, we are being blinded to the negative peer pressure we, as adults, succumb to each and every day.
Man's downfall was the result of lust:

<u>Genesis 3: 1-7</u>
3:1 "Now the serpent was more subtil than any beast of the field which the Lord God had made. And he said, Ye shall not eat of every tree of the garden"

3:2 "And the woman said unto the serpent, We may eat of the fruit of the trees of the garden:

3:3 "But of the fruit of the tree which is in the midst of the garden, God hath said, Ye shall not eat of it, neither shall ye touch it, lest ye die"

3:4 "And the serpent said unto the woman, Ye shall not surely die:

3:5 "For God doth know that in the day ye eat thereof, then your eyes shall be opened, and ye shall be as gods, knowing good and evil"

3:6 "And when the woman saw that the tree was good for food, and that it was pleasant to the eyes, and a tree to be desired to make one wise, she took of the fruit thereof, and did eat, and gave also unto her husband with her; and he did eat"

3:7 "And the eyes of them both were opened, and they knew they were naked; and they sewed fig leaves together, and made themselves aprons"

Lust entered in the moment Eve began to entertain the serpent. First the devil got into her head by contradicting God's instructions and once he had her attention he showed her the fruit. Despite the fact God had given Adam and Eve liberty to enjoy all the other trees in the garden, the devil, through the spirit of lust, used the one tree that was forbidden to draw them away from God. The moment the serpent contradicted (questioned) the commandment given to Adam and Eve by God; the conversation should have been cast down. The result of them listening to the reasoning of the serpent was the lust of flesh (she saw the tree was good), the lust of the eyes (it was pleasant to the eyes), and the pride of life (a tree to be desired to make one wise).

The psychology of the serpent (devil) is the same today. He uses compromise, complacency, justification, and reasoning to water down and contradict the commandments of God, and straying away from God's commandments opens the door. We must make a decision to adhere to God's commandments in order to be victorious. Adam and Eve had a choice. The serpent was powerless to force them to disobey God; the choice was solely in their hands.

Today we are still battling the choice between the feeble invitations of the devil versus having faith in God to provide us with abundant life. Many times we give in to the spirit of lust because we do not have the patience to wait on God.

The purpose of this chapter is to arm you with spiritual weaponry to identify and cast down the spirit of lust whenever it appears. Victory is essential in a day and age where lustful influences are the norm.

In the following passages contrast the manner in which Jesus Christ dealt with temptation to the way in which Adam and Eve did. Pay close attention to the outcome achieved by Jesus Christ through standing on the Word of God in the face of the psychology of the devil. Jesus did not reason with the devil, entertain his psychology, nor open the door to temptation. He remained steadfast and spoke the Word of God.

Matthew 4:1-11

4:1 "Then was Jesus led up of the Spirit into the wilderness to be tempted of the devil."

4:2 "And when He had fasted forty days and forty nights, He was afterward an hungered."

4:3 "And when the tempter came to Him, He said, If thou be the Son of God, command that these stones be made bread."

4:4 "But He answered and said, **It is written**, Man shall

not live by bread alone, but by every word that proceedeth out of the mouth of God."

4:5 "Then the devil taketh Him up into the holy city, and setteth Him on a pinnacle of the temple,"

4:6 "And saith unto Him, If thou be the Son of God, cast thyself down: for it is written, He shall give His angels charge concerning thee: and in their hands they shall bear thee up, lest at any time thou dash thy foot against a stone."

4:7 "Jesus said unto him, **It is written again**, Thou shalt not tempt the Lord thy God."

4:8 "Again, the devil taketh Him up into an exceeding high mountain, and sheweth Him all the kingdoms of the world, and the glory of them;"

4:9 "And saith unto Him, all these things will I give thee, if thou wilt fall down and worship me."

4:10 "Then saith Jesus unto him, **Get thee hence satan: for it is written**, Thou shalt worship the Lord thy God, and Him only shalt thou serve."

4:11 "Then the devil leaveth Him, and behold, angels came and ministered unto Him."

Consider the following example; same sex marriages.

The Bible is very clear on this issue. The Bible says that for the cause of marriage a man will leave his father and mother and cleave unto his wife and the two will become one. However, the more the premise of same sex marriage is entertained, the more we listen to the reasoning behind it. The more we see it on TV and other forms of media, the more we are desensitized. The more it is justified by religious leaders, the more we begin to change our perception about how to interpret what the Bible states.

To make matters worse, those that stand on what the Bible says are vilified and seen as politically incorrect hate mongers, whereas a short time ago you would have just been seen as a Bible believing Christian.

<u>Mark 10:6-9</u>
10:6 "But from the beginning of the creation God made them male and female."
10:7 "For this cause shall a man leave his father and mother, and cleave to his wife."
10:8 "And they twain shall be one flesh: so then they are no more twain, but one flesh."
10:9 "What therefore God hath joined together, let no man put asunder."

God's word has not changed on same sex relations but as society strays further away from God's word, the more we are willing to believe a lie, the same as Adam and Eve. The discussion should have been over at the "Word of God says...."

Lust can be subtle or overt, and the primary ways we allow it in is through the choices we make with our eyes and ears. You can't expect to have victory over the spirit of lust if you flood your mind with sexually explicit images, sexually explicit conversations, music or movies that are sexually explicit, pornography, or place yourselves in environments that are sexually charged. The types of situations and people you expose yourself to have a definite impact on the thoughts, feelings, and spirits that gain access to your mind. We have taken in so many lustful images it oftentimes becomes entrenched in our sexuality, and this is what opens the door for lust to brazenly walk right on in.

The Bible tells us by walking in the spirit we shall not fulfill the lust of the flesh. When you flood your mind with prayer, the word, and the things of God, the result will be healthy thoughts and feelings. You will be able to recognize the spirit of lust a mile away and have the strength to cast it down whenever it appears. The choice is yours, but one thing is for sure, your victory over the spirit of lust will be determined by whatever you flood your mind with.

I pray that as you read the following section the scriptures will become impressed upon your heart and mind and strengthen you in the battle to overcome lust. I added this chapter to the book because I am led to believe there are a significant number of professing Christians that still engage in fornication, adultery, the use of pornography and other forms of sexual immorality all stemming from the spirit of lust. This spirit can be broken in your life.

The Bible not only warns us concerning the spirit of lust, but the consequences as well.

<u>Proverbs 5:1-13</u>

5:1 "My son, attend unto my wisdom, and bow thine ear to my understanding:

5:2 "That thou mayest regard discretion, and that thy lips may keep knowledge:

5:3 "For the lips of a strange woman drop as an honeycomb, and her mouth is smoother than oil:

5:4 "But her end is bitter as wormwood, sharp as a two-edged sword:

5:5 "Her feet go down to death; her steps take hold on hell:

5:6 "Lest thou shouldest ponder the path of life, her ways are moveable, that thou canst not know them:

5:7 "Hear me now therefore, O ye children, and depart not from the words of my mouth:

5:8 "Remove thy way far from her, and come not nigh the door of her house:

5:9 "Lest thou give thine honour unto others, and thy years unto the cruel:

5:10 "Lest strangers be filled with thy wealth; and thy labors be in the house of a stranger:

5:11 "And thou mourn at the last, when thy flesh and thy body are consumed:

5:12 "And say. How have I hated instruction, and my heart-despised reproof?

5:13 "And have not obeyed the voice of my teachers, nor inclined my ear to them that instructed me"

The spirit of lust can cost you everything. It can strip you of your honor, reputation, authority, success, your career and family, your health and wealth, your life, and ultimately cost you your soul.

The Bible says you can enjoy the pleasures of sin for a season but the end result is death. Sin can be very attractive, pleasurable, and appealing to the eye, and overcoming sin is not based on feelings, rather it is a decision to live God's way, as opposed to the world's way, that is fueled by your love for Him.

The love of God keeps you faithful and His goodness, mercy, and grace, gives you the strength to resist the temptations of the world. This is not a one time fight. Daily you must line up with God's Word by taking heed to the wise counsel and warnings that are given in the scriptures. You must not view the Bible as a book of suggestions, but as your blueprint to success in every area of your life. It is made alive through an active prayer life that involves standing on God's word and declaring it back to Him.

<u>I Thessalonians 4:7</u> "For God has not called us unto uncleanness, but unto holiness"

<u>Hebrews 13:4</u> "Marriage is honorable in all, and the bed undefiled: but whoremongers and adulterers God will judge."

God does not forbid us from enjoying sex and affection, but He created sex for the confines of marriage. Sex can and should be enjoyed often in a marriage, but outside of marriage it is just another apple the serpent uses to draw us away from God. Once again God has given us a beautiful garden to enjoy and Satan seeks to distort God's plan by drawing us into disobedience. Sex outside of marriage is lust driven and a sin. The Bible says to enjoy the beauty and affection of your own spouse and be blessed by her bosom.

<u>I Corinthians 7:1-2</u>
7:1 "Now concerning the things whereof ye wrote unto me: It is good for a man not to touch a woman:
7:2 "Nevertheless, to avoid fornication, let every man have his own wife, and let every woman have her own husband"

This scripture does not advocate marrying the first woman that you see so that you can have sex. If you desire a companion or helpmate, then it is your responsibility to seek the face of the Lord, be patient, and allow God to help lead you to the companion that is right for you. If you have already found a companion, then you need to marry him/her and quit having sex until you're married. God is not moved by the phrase "we're going to get married." You're either married or you're fornicating.

There is so much more to marriage than just the sexual aspects, which would take another book to do the subject justice. The most important thing to know is that when God created man He wanted him to be just like Him. Marriage and sex are about saving your very best for someone very special that only he or she can enjoy. This is the same way that God shared His very best with us.

<u>II Timothy 2:22</u> "Flee also youthful lusts: but follow righteousness, faith, charity, peace, with them that call on the Lord out of a pure heart"

<u>Proverbs 5:15-20</u>
5:15 "Drink waters out of thine own cistern, and running waters out of thine own well:
5:16 "Let thy fountains be dispersed abroad, and rivers of waters in the streets:
5:17 "Let them be only thine own, and not strangers with thee:
5:18 "Let thy fountains be blessed: and rejoice with the wife of thy youth:
5:19 "Let her be as the loving hind and pleasant roe; let her breasts satisfy thee at all times; and be thou ravished always with her love:
5:20 "And why wilt thou, my son, be ravished with a strange woman, and embrace the bosom of a stranger?"

Sex outside of marriage can keep you from inheriting the kingdom of God.
<u>I. Corinthians 6:9</u> "Know ye not that the unrighteous

shall not inherit the kingdom of God? Be not deceived: neither **fornicators**, nor idolaters, nor **adulterers**, nor effeminate, nor abusers of themselves with mankind"

When you are tempted, either the flesh or the Spirit is going to rise up because fornication and adultery are workings of the flesh. The wonderful news is that any spirit that opposes God can be driven out if you are willing to repent and embrace the Word of God. If you have been feeding your Spirit man (Word of God, prayer, and a holy lifestyle), then you will have power to overcome the temptation. If you have been feeding your flesh (lustful thoughts/images, worldly influences), then your flesh will rise up and the result is being drawn away and enticed. The more you surround yourself with the things of God the more fortified you will be against attack. Despite what society says, fornication, lust, and adultery are sins and can be overcome. Unfortunately people tend to find comfort in numbers, and readily conform to the opinions of the masses. This justification will not hold up when you stand before God.

<u>I Corinthians 6:15-20</u>
6:15 "Know ye not that your bodies are the members of Christ? Shall I then take the members of Christ, and make them the members of a harlot? God forbid:
6:16 "What? Know ye not that he which is joined to an harlot is one body? For two, saith he, shall be one flesh:
6:17 "But he that is joined unto the Lord is one spirit:
6:18 "Flee fornication. Every sin that a man doeth is without the body; but he that committeth fornication sinneth against his own body:
6:19 "What? Know ye not that your body is the temple

of the Holy Ghost which is in you, which ye have of God, and ye are not your own?

6:20 "For ye are bought with a price: therefore glorify God in your body, and in your spirit, which are God's"

<u>Proverbs 6:26-32</u>
6:26 "For by means of a whorish woman a man is brought to a piece of bread: and the adulteress will hunt for the precious life:

6:27 "Can a man take fire in his bosom and his clothes not be burned?

6:28 "Can one go upon hot coals, and his feet not be burned?

6:29 "So he that goeth in to his neighbor's wife; whosoever toucheth her shall not be innocent:

6:30 "Men do not despise a thief, if he steal to satisfy his soul when he is hungry:

6:31 "But if he be found, he shall restore sevenfold, he shall give all the substance of his house:

6:32 "But whoso committeth adultery with a woman lacketh understanding: he that doeth it destroyeth his own soul:

The worldview and God's Word on sex are in direct opposition; however we are bombarded by the worldview on a daily basis. Society profits from sexuality, whether it is selling products, increasing ratings on television, or appealing to the flesh. This view is being shaped and reinforced everyday through the media, movies, music, billboards, magazines, lifestyles, and other influences we encounter each day. The more you are subjected to the worldview the easier it becomes to adopt the reasoning of the world and believe the lie.

The responsibility is solely that of the individual to seek

the Word of God and discover what God's instructions are and live by them. We find ourselves replaying the scenario in the garden on a daily basis, constantly faced with the choice to either end the conversation at **"The Word of God says."** or choosing to see what the serpent is showing us (lust of the eyes), considering the benefits, pleasures, and rewards (lust of the flesh), and making a decision to please ourselves as opposed to obeying God (pride of life).

Don't be fooled. The minute you start making the rules, you have just become your own God. You either live by God's commandments or by your own.

Once lust gains access to your mind, it is a cancer that begins to spread into your thoughts making it very difficult to get out. The line between what is normal and what is lust-driven slowly erodes and the thoughts become increasingly selfish and deviant. The whole notion of love is lost in a sea of self-gratification and hormonal impulse resulting in sin and death.

Death can be both physical and spiritual with various states of loss suffered in between. It can bring about depression, disease, loneliness, isolation, and other forms of emptiness associated with living outside of the will of God. Lust will take you places you never imagined, and each time you go you are robbed of your character, your innocence, your honor, and your integrity. When you return, you don't even recognize what you've become because you simply accept it as what you are. It begins to infect your prayer life and your conscience leaving you with feelings of guilt and hypocrisy. Lust always results in pain and alienation under the illusion of pleasure and conquest, and the more you flood your mind with societal views the more the illusion becomes your truth.

Those bound by lust are driven deeper and deeper

into its darkness resulting in dysfunctional relationships, hardened hearts, divorce, and sexual immorality. You begin to crave that which you cannot have and desire those things that appear to be in your reach. It is a hole that is never filled and a thirst that is never quenched. It is a mere carrot the devil dangles in front of you, always ahead of you, but never out of sight. You strive for satisfaction only to find it is even further out of your reach. The more dissatisfied you are, the more you search for new and more deviant things to fill the void. The answers seem to be somewhere in the darkness, but your search continues to come up empty. The thoughts of shame are short lived because the minute you turn on the TV, the radio, or the computer you are bombarded with a mountain of new adventures and roads that have yet to be traveled.

Proverbs 23:27 "For a whore is a deep ditch; and a strange woman is a narrow pit"

Proverbs 7:10, 21-27
7:10 "And, behold, there met him a woman with the attire of an harlot, and subtil of heart:

7:21 "With her much fair speech she caused him to yield, with the flattering of her lips she forced him:

7:22 "He goeth after her straightway, as an ox goeth to the slaughter, or as a fool to the correction of the stocks;

7:23 "Till a dart strike through his liver; as a bird hasteth to the snare, and knoweth not that it is for his life:

7:24 "Hearken unto me now therefore, O ye children, and attend to the words of my mouth:

7:25 "Let not thine heart decline to her ways, go not astray in her paths:

7:26 "For she hast cast down many wounded: yea, many strong men have been slain by her:

7:27 "Her house is the way to hell, going down to the chambers of death"

Make no mistake; there is nothing normal or innocent about sex outside of marriage and adultery. The devil has used seduction to destroy the lives of many. The seductress is always hunting and patiently waiting for her prey and you can't rely on will power and cold showers to defeat her. A holy lifestyle will drastically diminish the amount of lustful images you are exposed to and dull its influence on your life. The spirit of lust must make a connection with something on the inside and the more you fill your heart and mind with the things of God the more lust will have no place in you.

The best battles are the ones that you don't have to fight. A holy lifestyle will cause you to fight less, avoid many temptations, and keep you out of the wrong type of situations. The Bible instructs us to be separate from the world so that we can live quiet and peaceable lives. A lifestyle in the world will put you directly in harms way.

Jude 1:7 "Even as Sodom and Gomorrah, and the cities about them in like manner, giving themselves over to fornication, and going after strange flesh, are set forth for an example, suffering the vengeance of eternal fire"

Romans 6:12 "Let not sin therefore reign in your mortal body, that ye should obey it in the lusts thereof"

Ephesians 5:5 "For this ye know, that no whoremonger, nor unclean person, nor covetous man, who is an idolater, hath nay inheritance in the kingdom of Christ and of God"

The worldview glorifies free willed sexuality, whereas the Bible says that those that engage in sexual deviance will not inherit the kingdom of God.

<u>Romans 1:24-32</u>
1:24 "Wherefore God also gave them up to uncleanness through the lust of their own hearts, to dishonour their own bodies between themselves:

1:25 "Who changed the truth of God into a lie, and worshipped and served the creature more than the Creator, who is blessed for ever. Amen:

1:26 "For this cause God gave them up unto vile affections: for even their women did change the natural use into that which is against nature:

1:27 " And likewise also the men, leaving the natural use of the woman, burned in their lust one toward another; men with men working that which is unseemly, and receiving in themselves that recompense of their error which was meet:

1:28 "And even as they did not like to retain God in their knowledge, God gave them over to a reprobate mind, to do those things which are not convenient;

1:29 "Being filled with all unrighteousness, fornication, wickedness, covetousness, maliciousness; full of envy, murder, debate, malignity; whisperers,

1:30 "Backbiters, haters of God, despiteful, proud, boasters, inventors of evil things, disobedient to parents:

1:31 "Without understanding, covenant breakers, without natural affection, implacable, unmerciful:

1:32 "Who knowing the judgment of God, that they

which commit such things are worthy of death, not only do the same, but have pleasure in them that do them"

Sin is a slippery slope and the longer that you engage in sin the further you slide. It is a dangerous thing to ignore that still small voice on the inside that tells us (conviction) that we are wrong. That voice could be the only thing separating a person from facing the ultimate consequence of a life that is disobedient to God. Have you ever wondered why people engaged in deviant behavior spend so much time defending their choices and convincing others, including themselves, that their lifestyles are legitimate in the eyes of God? It's because of that still small voice. You either find a way to drown that voice out or it can become unbearable for most people. The reason why so many people suffer from anxiety and depression is because they are haunted by their conscience. That voice or conviction is the only thing that separates us from having a conscience (that feeling of knowing something is wrong) and having no conscience at all where sin is concerned.

Once you lose your conscience you become reprobate, having no boundaries or remorse, you simply do whatever feels good to satisfy your flesh whether it is right or wrong. The Bible warns us that you can ignore God (the still voice) to the point that you are no longer convicted of your sin. (Verse 1:28 above "God gave them over to a reprobate mind") Note the choice is not made by God; rather He simply ceases to convict the individual that makes a choice not to retain Him in his knowledge ("when you choose not to hear God's instruction and live by His Word").

God is not the one that sends a person to hell or causes them to become reprobate. When an individual says in his/her heart that the desire to engage in sin and live outside of God's commandments is more important than living by the Word of God, a decision has been made. Once you follow that decision, it is the consequences that result in sin and death. IT IS NOT AN ACT OF GOD.

James 1:14-15
1:14 "But every man is tempted, when he is drawn away of his own lust and enticed:
1:15 "Then when lust hath conceived, it bringeth forth sin: and sin, when it is finished, bringeth forth death"

God is not the tempter. The devil (serpent) is the tempter and has been tempting man since the Garden of Eden. Temptation will always be around. The issue is whether or not you are able to deal with the temptation when it comes. Men/Women are drawn away (they give in to the temptation) by conditions that exist already within their hearts/minds. As stated earlier, when you flood your heart/mind with lustful thoughts/images, the process of temptation has already begun. The point in which you realize that you are being tempted is merely a manifestation of conditions that were already in your heart/mind.

You cannot be ashamed to follow the examples of Christ even in the face of persecution, to think differently in light of the negative labels and slander you may endure, or to take a stand in the minority when it seems as if the world is standing against you. You must be willing to abstain when others are eager to participate, to speak out when your words may cause you to be ostracized, and to believe the Bible even when it is the unpopular thing to do. In other words, you must learn to be like Jesus.

Matthew 5:29-30
5:29 "And if thy right eye offend thee, pluck it out, and

cast it from thee: for it is profitable for thee that one of thy members should perish, and not that thy whole body should be cast into hell:

5:30 "And if thy right hand offend thee, cut it off, and cast it from thee: for it is profitable for thee that one of thy members should perish, and not that thy whole body should be cast into hell"

In other words do whatever it takes when it comes to dealing with the sin in your life. No person, possession, environment, or activity is worth losing your soul over. If there are sinful influences in your life, then cut them off without thinking twice about it. The examples used in the above scripture simply point out how far a person must be willing to go to battle sin. The Bible is not instructing people to mutilate themselves; rather it is illustrating the importance of walking away from anything that causes you to stumble. When you take your last breath, the only thing that is going to matter is your relationship with Jesus Christ and His Word. Standing before God is an individual appointment so you must make the best decision possible concerning the only thing that is going to matter. Don't spend time worrying about what people think; spend time lining yourself up with the Word of God.

Sin is a choice and you have been made free from the bondage of sin. Jesus Christ gives you the strength to make the right choice after you have availed yourself of His power through the word and prayer. The word is your anchor that allows you to bring your body into the subjection of your mind. You are in control of your life and not the carnal desires that attempt to taint your soul.

Romans 6:18-19

6:18 "Being then made free from sin, ye became the servants of righteousness:

6:19 "I speak after the manner of men because of the infirmity of your flesh: for as ye have yielded your members servants to uncleanness and to iniquity unto iniquity; even so now yield your members servants to righteousness unto holiness"

Jesus paid the price for sin on the cross so that we would not be bound by it. He paid the price for all that call upon His name and our lives are no longer our own. Yes, Jesus gave His own life for you! What are you willing to give up for Him?

<u>I Corinthians 6:19-20</u>
6:19 "What? Know ye not that your body is the temple of the Holy Ghost which is in you, which ye have of God, and ye are not your own?

6:20 "For ye are bought with a price: therefore glorify God in your body, and in your spirit, which are God's"

Make a decision right now to live holy:

Conclusion

The great news is everything discussed in this book can be summed up in one thought: "it's time to quit taking God's grace and mercy for granted." As Christians, we must come to the conclusion that God's gift is not cheapened by the fact that it is free. Playing on both sides of the fence will cost you everything. One may say, "Well what if you're wrong?" My response to that is "What if I'm right? Is your eternity worth gambling on?"

The bottom line is we are all born with something to surrender to God. The Bible says all men are born in sin and it is the very love of God that draws us out of sin through our acceptance of Jesus Christ. So the argument "I was born this way" is a valid point, however we are all born that way. We are all born into sin needing to die to our old nature and born again in His nature. One person may battle with homosexuality and the next person may battle with pride, but we are all born with something to surrender.

I. Timothy 1:15 "This is a faithful saying, and worthy of all acceptation, that Christ Jesus came into the world to save sinners; of whom I am chief"

I did not have to be taught how to sin; I merely had to be exposed to it. I was born with a predisposition to sin because sin was in me, and the more I was exposed to it the more I embraced it. I slept with many different women with no guilt or shame seeking only to satisfy the cravings of my flesh; I abused drugs and alcohol and enjoyed it. I flooded my mind with pornography and evil thoughts because it was entertaining. I adopted a street mentality because it was exciting. I have lied out of selfishness to avoid the consequences of my actions, and I have cheated because it was advantageous. I have lived outside of the will of God because I thought His will was boring, but through it all, it was the love of God that drew me to repentance. This is God's love in its purest form and He will do the same for anyone else that is willing to surrender.

The message of repentance is one of hope and freedom that is obtained through truth. At some point, I had to accept God's word and make a decision to either continue living the way I chose or seek the face of the Lord for deliverance. Needless to say, it was not an easy choice, and although the signs of deterioration were evident in my life, I clung to carnal vices with all of my heart. I lusted after the excitement of the streets and the more I tried to let go, the more I was driven further behind enemy lines. The biggest challenge was accepting God's word concerning who I was in Christ in the face of the feelings, desires, and thoughts I entertained that had become so familiar to me. In other words, by faith, I had to make a decision to accept what the word said about me even though my mind and body told me I was the man I saw in the mirror each day, the man that lusted to be a part of the world. It was the grace and love of God that delivered me from the sinful nature I was trapped in, but only after I made a choice to accept the fact I was living outside of the will of God. I then adopted His standard by which to live my life. That my friend is the love of God and it is a beautiful thing. Had I chosen to reject God's commandment in order to hold onto my own ways, it would not have been the love of God that sent me to hell.

The Lord continues to share His love with me in many different ways and the more I dwell in His love the stronger I become. His love does not always make sense, nor does it always seem fair, but it is a supernatural transfer built on trust and faith in Him. I learned His love is unselfish not neglectful, and when things don't happen according to my time frame I must also remember that He loves other people besides me. It's not always about me when it comes to the things of God and sometimes my life is more about being a blessing than it is about how much God can bless me.

One way the Lord taught me this valuable lesson of unselfish love was by instructing me to minister to a homeless population over the past few years. This involved feeding, clothing, and having Bible study with them. At first I felt very good about how the Lord was using me. I saw it as a one sided exchange in which I was making sacrifices to assist a population of people living deep in the trenches of the city. Many of them had been there for years and I often wondered how they managed to survive week after week given the elements they were subjected to. They would huddle together in corners, near vents, against walls, and other open spaces. They had the stench of the street on their clothes, bad hygiene, and many reeked of alcohol and urine. It was very apparent several of them were using drugs and it was sometimes very challenging to reach out and embrace them given the condition they were in. They would oftentimes attempt to take advantage of me in order to get money for their drugs and alcohol habits. Some even made intimidating demands and others did not bother to say thank you.

The more the Lord sent me down to minister to them the more He began to show me my real purpose in being there was to be ministered to. As I looked into their faces, the Lord began to define for me what His love was all about. He allowed me to see what it truly meant to love while expecting nothing in return. It was the purest form of love that I had ever experienced. I was a servant in every sense of the word sent down there to simply minister to the needs of God's people. Although society had forgotten about them, they were still special to God, and regardless how far they may have sunk in life, they were still within His reach. God's love is so strong that if they lived underground He would have simply provided me with a shovel.

The Lord instructed me to look past their appearance each time I embrace them with a hug, continue feeding them although they could offer me absolutely nothing in return, look past their habits, lifestyles, and sin, and to see something special in them many of them could not even see in themselves. He wanted me to see the destructive effects of sin while having compassion and mercy on those that were bound by it.

I had no measure by which to gauge my progress, and oftentimes I would find them in the same condition I left them in the week before, but the Lord told me not to get weary and never give up on them. Every time I got frustrated, the Lord reminded me He never gave up on loving me. You see, it had nothing to do with my notion of progress or success when it came to the will of God. There was no one down there to pat me on the back, no certificates or awards to be earned, or any other honors from men. It was simply about making the love of God available. It didn't matter to God whether or not I saw any progress; He simply wanted His people to know He loved them. It didn't matter if they stuck around to listen to what I had to say or if they even read the tracts. The love was unconditional with no strings attached. You see, the love of God is free but salvation is a choice. Who will you choose? Will you choose the gods of this world that offer instant gratification and death, or the God of Abraham, Isaac, and Jacob who guarantees eternal life?

A Message to Christians

I. Corinthians 10:1-10

10:1 "Moreover, brethren, I would not that ye should be ignorant, how that all our fathers were under the cloud, and all passed through the sea;

10:2 "And were all baptized unto Moses in the cloud and in the sea;

10:3 "And did all eat the same spiritual meat;

10:4 "And did all drink the same spiritual drink: for they drank of that spiritual Rock that followed them: and that rock was Christ."

10:5 "But with many of them God was not well pleased: for they were overthrown in the wilderness."

10:6 "Now these things were our examples, to the intent we should not lust after evil things, as they also lusted."

10:7 "Neither be ye idolaters, as were some of them; as it is written, The people sat down to eat and drink, and rose up to play."

10:8 "Neither let us commit fornication, as some of them committed, and fell in one day three and twenty thousand."

10:9 "Neither let us tempt Christ, as some of them also tempted, and were destroyed of serpents."

10:10 "Neither murmur ye, as some of them also murmured, and were destroyed of the destroyer."

We are all reading the same book but not receiving the same instruction. We are serving the same Holy God but not following the same Holy covenant. We all claim to love Jesus but many refuse to keep His commandments. We have all been warned concerning the lust of the world but so many of us still choose to remain in it. The power is available yet there are many that are not filled with it.

God is not well pleased. The title "Christian" is not a shield from the judgment of God the same as the children of Israel could not hide behind the covenant when they refused to live by God's instruction. The covenant must be in your heart. Grace is not a rocking chair to make you comfortable. The time is now to repent and turn away from all iniquity. The Lord is gracious and His mercy everlasting. He is ready to forgive you and wash the slate clean, but only if you make a sincere decision to repent and live by His Word. I urge you not to miss this opportunity or allow these words to fall on deaf ears. Open up your heart and allow the grace of God to invade the empty areas of your life. You are reading this book for a reason and a purpose that was determined for you before I ever picked up the pen. God works through people and He is working through this book in order to talk to you. Make a decision right now to line up with His will for your life. Have the faith to let go of those things that displease Him and He will do the rest. I say to you once again to make a decision right now. An altar is not required to make this commitment and you do not have to wait to get back to church. Open your mouth and begin to speak right where you are and God will hear you. Simply start by saying I'm sorry Lord and your heart will do the rest. God loves you and it is not His will that any man perishes but that all should come to repentance!

Made in the USA